pfSense 2 Cookbook

A practical, example-driven guide to configure even the
most advanced features of pfSense 2

Matt Williamson

BIRMINGHAM - MUMBAI

pfSense 2 Cookbook

Copyright © 2011 Packt Publishing

First published: March 2011

Production Reference: 1180311

Published by Packt Publishing Ltd.
32 Lincoln Road
Olton
Birmingham, B27 6PA, UK.

ISBN 978-1-849514-86-6

www.packtpub.com

Cover Image by Asher Wishkerman (a.wishkerman@mpic.de)

Credits

Author
Matt Williamson

Reviewers
Josh Brower
Jim Cheetham
Brad Hedlund
Mohd Izhar Bin Ali

Acquisition Editor
Tarun Singh

Development Editor
Alina Lewis

Technical Editor
Krutika V. Katelia

Indexer
Monica Ajmera Mehta
Rekha Nair

Editorial Team Leader
Akshara Aware

Project Team Leader
Priya Mukherji

Project Coordinator
Jovita Pinto

Proofreader
Kevin Mcgowan

Production Coordinator
Alwin Roy

Cover Work
Alwin Roy

About the Author

Matt Williamson is the founder of Blue Key Consulting, a software design and development firm located in the New York City area. Prior to starting his consulting business, Matt worked as a software developer for various insurance and financial companies in Chicago and New York. Matt can be reached through his personal website at http://www.bunkerhollow.com.

About the Reviewers

Josh Brower has been working in IT since he crashed his first computer at age 14. He writes blogs regularly at `http://defensivedepth.com/` on a variety of Information Security topics. He is currently working with a non-profit organization as the head of IT Security, and pursuing his graduation degree in Information Security from STI. Josh is happily married to his wife Mandi. They have one son.

Jim Cheetham has been managing, deploying, supporting, and designing Unix solutions and TCP/IP networks for over 20 years. During this time, he has been part of the establishment of the first SSL-protected website outside the USA, the design and implementation of a high-volume web portal that deliberately had no firewalls between it and the Internet, and has run a busy Managed Network and Security Service looking after multiple government departments.

Jim has worked for global companies such as ICL, Vodafone, and Unisys, along with keeping hands-on with numerous small, interesting, and fast-moving businesses. Jim is currently running Inode Ltd., a New Zealand-based consultancy and service provider specializing in open source solutions for management of networks, systems, and security.

> I'd like to thank my wife Maria and my children Alexander and Katherine for letting me spend so much time behind the keyboard hacking, and for keeping things running smoothly at home when I have to take trips away for work.

Brad Hedlund is a Technical Solutions Architect at Cisco Systems, Inc. in the company's Center of Excellence for Data Center field sales. Since joining Cisco in 2006, Brad has been helping Enterprise customers design large and small data centers with challenging and complex requirements. Brad has extensive design experience with Cisco's Data Center switching line (Nexus) and Cisco's Unified Computing System (UCS), with specific expertise in server networking and virtualization. Brad Hedlund also maintains a popular blog on data center networking topics at `http://bradhedlund.com`.

Mohd Izhar Bin Ali, CEH CHFI is an independent security consultant having 10 years' working experience in networking, open source, and the IT Security field. He started his career as a Security Analyst with SCAN Associates, Berhad, and he is one of the team members managing the security services of an Intrusion Detection System (IDS) for Malaysian government's SOC center. After that, he became a trainer (LINUX and Networking) for the largest private education college in Malaysia. Before becoming a freelance security consultant, he worked with FIRMUS Security Sdn Bhd, one of the largest IT security companies in Malaysia. With FIRMUS, he had performed enterprise security assessment to clients (banking, insurance, and government) including web penetration testing, external and internal penetration testing, and wireless penetration testing. Now, takes up freelance jobs in security and also research in the network security field.

He has contributed articles on pfSense (*Setup Squid as A Transparent Proxy*, *Setup VideoCache with Squid*) and has also written white papers for The Exploit Database (MySQL Injection using `darkMySQLi.py`, Howto: DNS Enumeration, Easy Method: Blind SQL Injection).

I would like to thank Allah, my parents, my girlfriend Umairah, and also my best friend in IT security, Mohd Asrullita bin Abdul Taib.

www.PacktPub.com

Support files, eBooks, discount offers and more

You might want to visit www.PacktPub.com for support files and downloads related to your book.

Did you know that Packt offers eBook versions of every book published, with PDF and ePub files available? You can upgrade to the eBook version at www.PacktPub.com and as a print book customer, you are entitled to a discount on the eBook copy. Get in touch with us at service@packtpub.com for more details.

At www.PacktPub.com, you can also read a collection of free technical articles, sign up for a range of free newsletters and receive exclusive discounts and offers on Packt books and eBooks.

http://PacktLib.PacktPub.com

Do you need instant solutions to your IT questions? PacktLib is Packt's online digital book library. Here, you can access, read and search across Packt's entire library of books.

Why Subscribe?

- ▶ Fully searchable across every book published by Packt
- ▶ Copy & paste, print and bookmark content
- ▶ On demand and accessible via web browser

Free Access for Packt account holders

If you have an account with Packt at www.PacktPub.com, you can use this to access PacktLib today and view nine entirely free books. Simply use your login credentials for immediate access.

Instant Updates on New Packt Books

Get notified! Find out when new books are published by following @PacktEnterprise on Twitter, or the Packt Enterprise Facebook page.

To the important people in my life;
Alex, Paul, Deb, and Ted.
And to those who have lived and died fighting for my right to live my life any way I choose.

Table of Contents

Preface

pfSense is an open source distribution of FreeBSD-based firewall which provides a platform for flexible and powerful routing and firewalling. The versatility of pfSense presents us with a wide array of configuration options which, compared to other offerings, makes determining requirements a little more difficult and a lot more important. Through this book, you will see that pfSense offers numerous other alternatives to fit any environment's security needs.

This book follows a cookbook style to teach you how to use the features available with pfSense after determining your environment's security requirements. It covers everything from initial configuration of your network interfaces and pfSense services such as DHCP and Dynamic DNS to complex techniques to enable failover and load-balancing.

What this book covers

Chapter 1, Initial Configuration covers the settings needed for almost every pfSense deployment including those for a firewall, router, and wireless access point. Through the recipes in this chapter, you will learn how to install and configure pfSense with a fully-operational firewall and router.

Chapter 2, Essential Services explains how to configure the essential networking services provided by pfSense such as the DHCP server and dynamic DNS services.

Chapter 3, General Configuration describes how to configure NAT and firewall rules and the features associated with them.

Chapter 4, Virtual Private Networking describes how to configure pfSense to serve any or all of the four major VPN implementations—IPSec, L2TP, OpenVPN, and PPTP.

Chapter 5, Advanced Configuration covers advanced networking features such as configuring different types of virtual IP, creating gateways, and bridging interfaces.

Chapter 6, Redundancy, Load Balancing, and Failover contains recipes explaining how to load-balance or failover the multi-WAN interfaces to protect large and sensitive systems.

Chapter 7, Services and Maintenance describes all the networking services and features offered in pfSense such as configuring external logging (syslog server), enabling Wake On LAN (WOL), and configuring automatic configuration file backup.

Appendix A, Monitoring and Logging includes the features available in pfSense to help you monitor your system and also covers how to use different logging tools built into pfSense.

Appendix B, Determining our Hardware Requirements will show you how to choose the best pfSense configuration after you determine your firewall requirements. You will even learn how and where to deploy pfSense to fit your environment's security needs.

What you need for this book

A working installation of pfSense 2.0 is the only requirement for the recipes in this book. Readers who are new to pfSense can follow the recipes in the appendices for instructions on how to determine what type of hardware they should install pfSense on. The minimum requirements for a pfSense installation are 500Mhz, 128MB RAM, and 1GB hard disk space. PfSense can also be installed as a virtual machine, and for convenience a VMWare image is available from the **Downloads** section of the pfSense website.

Who this book is for

This book is intended for all levels of network administrators. If you are an advanced user of pfSense, then you can flip to a particular recipe and quickly accomplish the task at hand, while if you are new to pfSense, you can read chapter-by-chapter and learn all of the features of the system from the ground-up.

Conventions

In this book, you will find a number of styles of text that distinguish between different kinds of information. Here are some examples of these styles, and an explanation of their meaning.

Code words in text are shown as follows: "Our public key is now located at `/home/user/.ssh/id_rsa.pub`."

Any command-line input **or** output is written as follows:

```
ssh -i /home/matt/key/id_rsa admin@192.168.1.1
```

New terms and **important words** are shown in bold. Words that you see on the screen, in menus or dialog boxes for example, appear in the text like this: "On the **Virtual IPs** tab, click the "plus" button to add a new virtual IP Address".

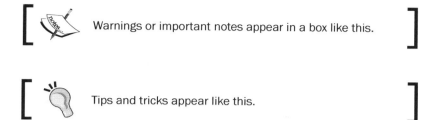

Warnings or important notes appear in a box like this.

Tips and tricks appear like this.

Reader feedback

Feedback from our readers is always welcome. Let us know what you think about this book—what you liked or may have disliked. Reader feedback is important for us to develop titles that you really get the most out of.

To send us general feedback, simply send an e-mail to `feedback@packtpub.com`, and mention the book title via the subject of your message.

If there is a book that you need and would like to see us publish, please send us a note in the **SUGGEST A TITLE** form on `www.packtpub.com` or e-mail `suggest@packtpub.com`.

If there is a topic that you have expertise in and you are interested in either writing or contributing to a book, see our author guide on www.packtpub.com/authors.

Customer support

Now that you are the proud owner of a Packt book, we have a number of things to help you to get the most from your purchase.

Errata

Although we have taken every care to ensure the accuracy of our content, mistakes do happen. If you find a mistake in one of our books—maybe a mistake in the text or the code—we would be grateful if you would report this to us. By doing so, you can save other readers from frustration and help us improve subsequent versions of this book. If you find any errata, please report them by visiting `http://www.packtpub.com/support`, selecting your book, clicking on the **errata submission form** link, and entering the details of your errata. Once your errata are verified, your submission will be accepted and the errata will be uploaded on our website, or added to any list of existing errata, under the Errata section of that title. Any existing errata can be viewed by selecting your title from `http://www.packtpub.com/support`.

Piracy

Piracy of copyright material on the Internet is an ongoing problem across all media. At Packt, we take the protection of our copyright and licenses very seriously. If you come across any illegal copies of our works, in any form, on the Internet, please provide us with the location address or website name immediately so that we can pursue a remedy.

Please contact us at copyright@packtpub.com with a link to the suspected pirated material.

We appreciate your help in protecting our authors, and our ability to bring you valuable content.

Questions

You can contact us at questions@packtpub.com if you are having a problem with any aspect of the book, and we will do our best to address it.

1
Initial Configuration

In this chapter, we will cover:

- ▶ Applying basic settings in General Setup
- ▶ Identifying and assigning interfaces
- ▶ Configuring the WAN interface
- ▶ Configuring the LAN interface
- ▶ Configuring optional interfaces
- ▶ Enabling the Secure Shell (SSH)
- ▶ Generating authorized RSA keys
- ▶ Configuring SSH RSA key authentication
- ▶ Accessing the Secure Shell (SSH)

Introduction

PfSense is an open source operating system used to turn a computer into a firewall, router, or a variety of other application-specific network appliances. PfSense is a customized FreeBSD distribution based on the **m0n0wall project**, a powerful but light-weight firewall distribution. PfSense builds upon m0n0wall's foundation and takes its functionality several steps further by adding a variety of other popular networking services.

This chapter covers the core settings needed for almost every pfSense deployment; whether that is a firewall, router, or even a wireless access point! Once pfSense is installed and configured according to the recipes in this chapter, you will have a fully-operation firewall plus router. At its most basic level, a pfSense machine can be used to replace the common home router when more functionality is desired. In more advanced configurations, pfSense can be used to establish a secure tunnel to a remote office, load-balance a web farm, or shape and prioritize all network traffic just to name a few example scenarios. There are literally hundreds of ways to configure and customize a pfSense installation.

Once pfSense is installed, there are two ways to access the system remotely—SSH and the WebGUI. An SSH connection will present you with the same low-level system menu that you would see on the screen if your machine is connected to a monitor. The SSH menu options are basic and very little configuration is done here. The entire configuration described in every recipe in this book is done through the WebGUI interface, unless specified otherwise, which is accessible through the IP address of any interface you configured during installation (such as 192.168.1.1).

Applying basic settings in General Setup

This recipe describes how to configure the core system settings in PfSense.

Getting ready

All that's required for this recipe is a base installation of pfSense and access to the WebGUI. Some of these settings will have been configured during the installation process, but can be modified here at any time.

> On a new install, the default credentials are:
> Username: admin
> Password: pfsense

How to do it...

1. Browse to **System | General Setup**.

2. Enter a **Hostname**. This name will be used to access the machine by name instead of the IP address. For example, we can browse to http://pfsense instead of http://192.168.1.1:

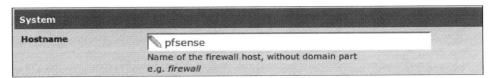

3. Enter your **Domain**:

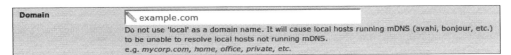

4. **DNS Servers** can be specified here. By default, pfSense will act as the primary DNS server and these fields will be blank. However, other DNS servers may certainly be used. Please refer to the *Specifying alternate DNS servers* recipe in *Chapter 2, Essential Services* for more information.

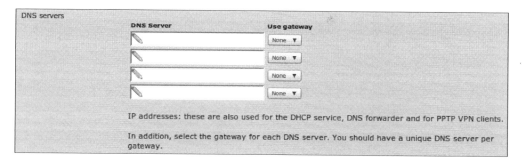

5. Check **Allow DNS server list to be overridden by DHCP/PPP on WAN**. This ensures that any DNS requests that can't be resolved internally are passed on and resolved by the external DNS servers provided by your ISP.

6. Enter a **Time zone** and leave the default **NTP time server** as **0.pfsense.pool.ntp.org**.

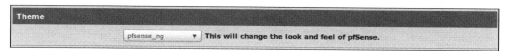

7. I'd recommend the default **Theme**, pfSense 2.0's new **pfsense_ng**. The top menus are now static and won't disappear if you scroll down through the content of the page, a great addition to the UI.

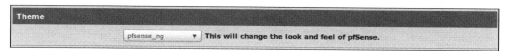

See also

▶ The *Configuring the DNS Forwarder* recipe in *Chapter 2, Essential Services*

▶ The *Specifying alternate DNS servers* recipe in *Chapter 2, Essential Services*

Identifying and assigning interfaces

This recipe describes how to identify a network configuration and assign the appropriate interfaces in pfSense.

Getting ready

You'll need to identify the MAC address for each Ethernet port on your pfSense machine before attempting to assign interfaces.

How to do it...

1. Access the console from the physical machine or enable SSH and connect remotely (see the *Enabling the Secure Shell (SSH)* recipe for details).

2. The home screen will display a list of interfaces, network ports, and IP addresses:

```
matt@thinkpad:~$ ssh admin@192.168.1.1
Password:
*** Welcome to pfSense 2.0-BETA5-nanobsd (i386) on pfsense ***

  WAN (wan)                -> fxp0         ->                 (DHCP)
  LAN (lan)                -> em0          -> 192.168.1.1
  OPT1 (opt1)              -> em1          -> NONE

  0) Logout (SSH only)              8) Shell
  1) Assign Interfaces              9) pfTop
  2) Set interface(s) IP address   10) Filter Logs
  3) Reset webConfigurator password 11) Restart webConfigurator
  4) Reset to factory defaults     12) pfSense Developer Shell
  5) Reboot system                 13) Upgrade from console
  6) Halt system                   14) Disable Secure Shell (sshd)
  7) Ping host

Enter an option:
```

3. Choose option **1** to **Assign Interfaces**.

4. Skip setting up VLANs for now. See the *Creating a Virtual LAN* recipe in *Chapter 5, Essential Services* for more information.

```
Enter an option: 1


Valid interfaces are:

em0   00:90:0b:12:01:52   (up)   Intel(R) PRO/1000 Network Connection 7.1.8
em1   00:90:0b:12:01:51   (down)        Intel(R) PRO/1000 Network Connection 7.1
.8
em2   00:90:0b:12:01:50   (down)        Intel(R) PRO/1000 Network Connection 7.1
.8
em3   00:90:0b:12:01:4f   (down)        Intel(R) PRO/1000 Network Connection 7.1
.8
fxp0  00:90:0b:12:01:53   (up)   Intel 82562ET/EZ/GT/GZ PRO/100 VE Ethernet

Do you want to set up VLANs first?

If you are not going to use VLANs, or only for optional interfaces, you should
say no here and use the webConfigurator to configure VLANs later, if required.

Do you want to set up VLANs now [y|n]? n
```

5. Assign each interface to the interface of your choice by matching the MAC address to the interface address on the display:

```
*NOTE*  pfSense requires *AT LEAST* 1 assigned interfaces to function.
        If you do not have *AT LEAST* 1 interfaces you CANNOT continue.

        If you do not have at least 1 *REAL* network interface cards
        or one interface with multiple VLANs then pfSense
        *WILL NOT* function correctly.

If you do not know the names of your interfaces, you may choose to use
auto-detection. In that case, disconnect all interfaces now before
hitting 'a' to initiate auto detection.

Enter the WAN interface name or 'a' for auto-detection: fxp0

Enter the LAN interface name or 'a' for auto-detection
NOTE: this enables full Firewalling/NAT mode.
(or nothing if finished): em0

Optional interface 1 description found: OPT1
Enter the Optional 1 interface name or 'a' for auto-detection
(or nothing if finished): em1

Enter the Optional 2 interface name or 'a' for auto-detection
(or nothing if finished):

The interfaces will be assigned as follows:

LAN  -> em0
WAN  -> fxp0
OPT1 -> em1

Do you want to proceed [y|n]?y

Writing configuration...done.
```

The ability to only configure a single interface is new to pfSense 2.0. Prior versions required a minimum of two (WAN and LAN) interfaces.

How it works...

pfSense, like any other computer operating system, references each NIC by some unique value (*fxp0, em0, em1*, and so on). These unique identifiers are often associated with the driver being used and make it easier for us humans to use than the associated MAC address (*00:80:0c:12:01:52*). Taking that concept a step further, an interface is simply a named placeholder for each port: *fxp0=WAN, em0=LAN, em1=DMZ*, and so on.

There's more...

Now that you know which port is mapped to which interface, you can manage future interface changes through the WebGUI by browsing to **Interfaces | (assign)**.

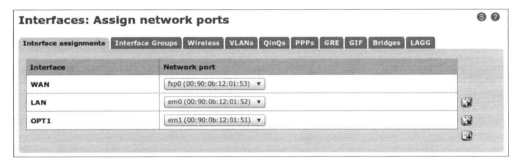

See also

 ▸ The *Accessing the Secure Shell (SSH)* recipe

 ▸ The *Configuring the WAN interface* recipe

 ▸ The *Configuring the LAN interface* recipe

 ▸ The *Configuring optional interfaces* recipe

Configuring the WAN interface

This recipe describes how to configure the **Wide Area Network** (**WAN**) on the external interface of our firewall.

Getting ready

The WAN interface is your connection to the outside world. You'll need a properly configured WAN interface (as described in the previous chapter) and an Internet connection. In this example, a cable modem provides the Internet connection from our local **Internet Service Provider** (**ISP**), but pfSense will support every other major connection method.

How to do it...

1. Browse to **Interfaces | WAN**.
2. Check **Enable Interface**.
3. Choose an address configuration **Type**.
4. Leave **MAC address** blank. Manually entering a MAC address here is known as "spoofing". Your ISP has no way of verifying MAC addresses, so you can simply make one up. This can be helpful if you're trying to force your ISP to hand you a new IP address or a different set of DNS servers.
5. Leave **MTU**, **MSS**, **Hostname**, and **Alias IP address** blank.

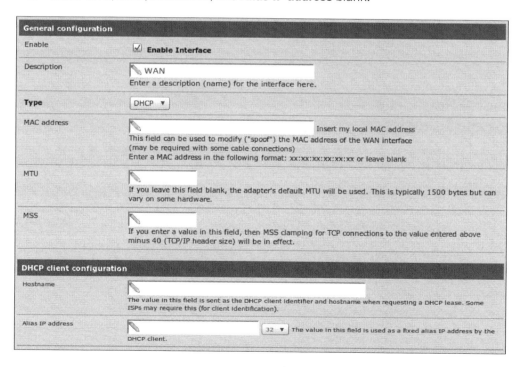

6. Check **Block private networks**. This setting is usually only checked on a WAN interface.

7. Check **Block bogon networks**. This setting is usually only checked on a WAN interface.

8. **Save** changes.

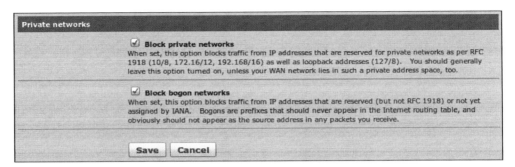

How it works...

We must first establish our connection to the Internet before we can configure pfSense to allow our other networks to access it. The example we've performed is typical of many SOHO environments. By placing our firewall as the only machine with direct access to the Internet, we are securing our environment by establishing complete control over the traffic that flows in and out of our networks. All traffic must now pass through our firewall and abide by our rules.

There's more...

We can now connect our WAN device (cable modem) to the WAN Ethernet port we've defined on our pfSense box. Once the connection has been established, we can check the status of our WAN port from **Status | Interfaces**:

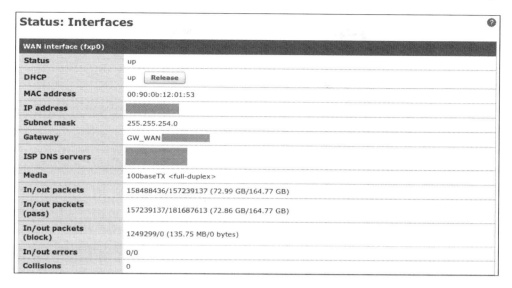

Status: Interfaces

WAN interface (fxp0)	
Status	up
DHCP	up [Release]
MAC address	00:90:0b:12:01:53
IP address	
Subnet mask	255.255.254.0
Gateway	GW_WAN
ISP DNS servers	
Media	100baseTX <full-duplex>
In/out packets	158488436/157239137 (72.99 GB/164.77 GB)
In/out packets (pass)	157239137/181687613 (72.86 GB/164.77 GB)
In/out packets (block)	1249299/0 (135.75 MB/0 bytes)
In/out errors	0/0
Collisions	0

See also

- ▶ The *Identifying and assigning interfaces* recipe
- ▶ The *Configuring the LAN interface* recipe
- ▶ The *Configuring optional interfaces* recipe

Configuring the LAN interface

This recipe describes how to configure the **Local Area Network** (**LAN**) internal interface of our firewall.

Getting ready

The LAN interface is used to connect your devices to a secure internal network. A properly configured LAN interface is required.

How to do it...

1. Browse to **Interfaces | LAN**.
2. Check **Enable Interface**.
3. Choose an address configuration **Type**.

4.   Enter an **IP address** and subnet mask. Leave **Gateway** set to **None**.

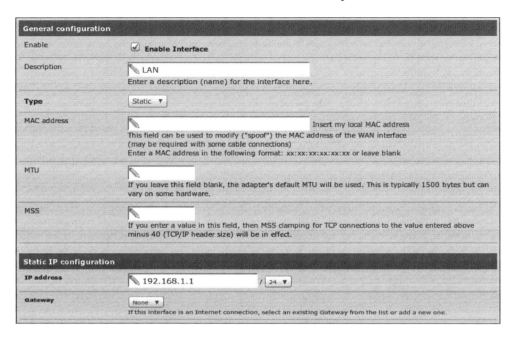

5.   Ensure **Block private networks** and **Block bogon networks** are **unchecked**.

6.   **Save** the changes.

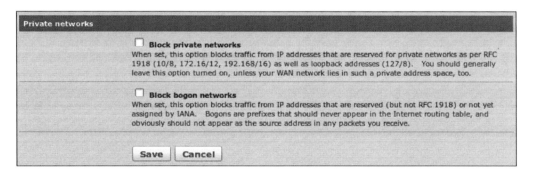

How it works...

You've just defined your first internal network. If you've been performing the recipes in order, you've now met the minimum requirements for a fully-functioning firewall! You've defined one external network (WAN) and one internal network (LAN). You can now define the rules and relationships to regulate traffic between the two.

There's more...

You can now connect a switch to the LAN interface on your pfSense machine. This will allow you to connect multiple computers to your LAN network.

See also

- ▸ The *Identifying and assigning interfaces* recipe
- ▸ The *Configuring the WAN interfaces* recipe
- ▸ The *Configuring optional interfaces* recipe

Configuring optional interfaces

This recipe describes how to create and assign optional network interfaces to our firewall.

Getting ready

The optional network you'll create in this is example is commonly referred to as a DMZ. The idea is taken from the military concept of a de-militarized zone, in which some traffic is allowed to pass and some traffic isn't. The idea is that the area is controlled and clearly separate from your other areas. When applied to networking, a DMZ network follows this pattern:

Internet Traffic | ← DMZ ← LAN Traffic

Unsafe Internet traffic is allowed to enter the DMZ, to access a webserver for example. LAN traffic can also enter the DMZ; it wants to access the webserver too. However, the key lies in the last rule—no DMZ traffic is allowed to enter the LAN.

The DMZ network is our less secure network we'll allow certain external access to. To configure a DMZ, or any other optional network, we'll need an available interface.

How to do it...

1. Browse to an available interface, **Interfaces | OPT1**.
2. Check **Enable Interface**.
3. Set **Description** to **DMZ**.
4. Choose an address configuration **Type**, **Static** for our example.
5. Enter an **IP address** and the subnet mask. We'll use **192.168.2.1** and select **24** from the drop-down list.

6. Leave **Gateway** set to **None**.

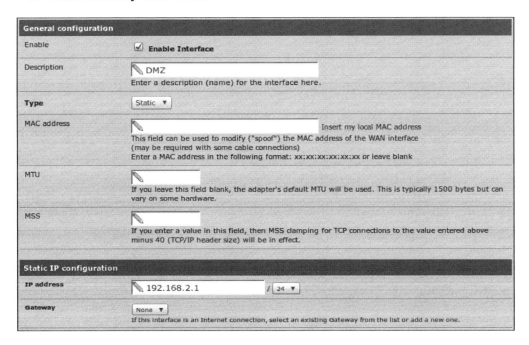

7. Ensure **Block private networks** and **Block bogon networks** are unchecked.
8. **Save** the changes.

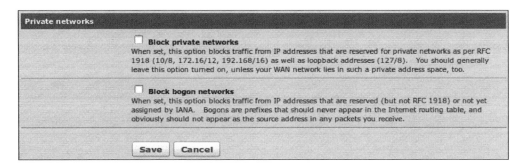

9. **Apply** changes.

How it works...

Your DMZ network will allow external (WAN) access. Your DMZ will also allow access from the LAN, but it won't be permitted to send traffic to the LAN. This will allow devices on the Internet to access your DMZ resources (websites, e-mail, and so on) without being able to access any part of your private LAN network.

There's more...

You could now attach a switch to your DMZ interface to connect multiple machines. If you've been following these recipes in order, a diagram of your network would look something like this:

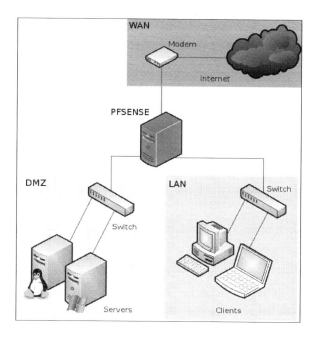

See also

- ▶ The *Identifying and assigning interfaces* recipe
- ▶ The *Configuring the WAN interface* recipe
- ▶ The *Configuring the LAN interface* recipe

Enabling the Secure Shell (SSH)

This recipe describes how to enable the Secure Shell (SSH) service in pfSense.

Getting ready

SSH is a networking protocol that allows encrypted communication between two devices. Enabling SSH allows secure access to the pfSense console remotely, just as if you were sitting in front of the physical console.

How to do it...

1. Browse to **System | Advanced | Secure Shell**.
2. Check **Enable Secure Shell**.
3. You will be prompted for credentials when you connect (use the same username and password as the webGUI), but checking **Disable password login for Secure Shell** will allow you to use RSA keys instead. See the next recipe for details.
4. Leave the **SSH port** blank to use the default port:

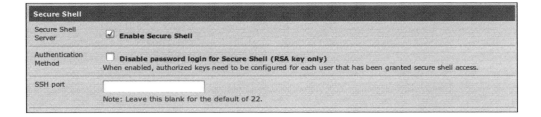

5. **Save** the changes and the SSH service will be started.

How it works...

Enabling the Secure Shell turns on pfSense's built-in SSH server to listen to requests on the port you've specified (port 22 by default).

 Like all pfSense services (unless otherwise noted), the SSH service will listen on every available interface. Like other services, firewall's rules are used to grant or deny access to these services. See *Chapter 3, General Configuration* for more information on configuring firewall rules.

There's more...

Changing the SSH authentication method to use RSA keys is a great way to secure access to your system. See the following recipe for details.

Additionally, you can change the port that SSH listens on. Doing so may increase security slightly by reducing the number of unauthorized login attempts, but you will need to remember what you have changed it to, or you will be unable to connect.

See also

▶ The *Generating authorized RSA keys* recipe

▶ The *Creating a firewall rule* recipe in *Chapter 3, General Configuration*

Generating authorized RSA keys

This recipe describes how to create an authorized RSA key so a user can connect to pfSense without being prompted for a password.

Getting ready

Linux and Mac users will need to ensure **ssh-keygen** is installed on their system (almost all distributions have this installed by default). Windows users will need to download and install the **PuTTYGen** tool.

How to do it...

Generate an SSH key from a Linux/Mac Client as follows:

1. Open a terminal and run:

   `ssh-keygen`

2. Save the key to the default location of `/home/user/.ssh/` and specify a pass code (optional, but recommended).

3. Your public key is now located at `/home/user/.ssh/id_rsa.pub`.

```
matt@thinkpad: ~
matt@thinkpad:~$ ssh-keygen
Generating public/private rsa key pair.
Enter file in which to save the key (/home/matt/.ssh/id_rsa):
Enter passphrase (empty for no passphrase):
Enter same passphrase again:
Your identification has been saved in /home/matt/.ssh/id_rsa.
Your public key has been saved in /home/matt/.ssh/id_rsa.pub.
The key fingerprint is:
21:34:73:68:8a:f2:e4:ec:14:81:90:47:b4:0b:1f:1d matt@thinkpad
The key's randomart image is:
+--[ RSA 2048]----+
|o=o E +..        |
|o oo oo+         |
|..oo.o. .        |
|.o+o.  . .       |
| *o.    S        |
|  =              |
|  o              |
|   .             |
|                 |
+-----------------+
matt@thinkpad:~$
```

Generate an SSH key from a Windows client using PuTTY as follows:

4. Open PuTTYGen and generate a public/private key pair by clicking the **Generate** button.

5. Enter a passphrase (optional, but recommended).

6. Click the **Save Private Key** button and choose a location, such as `C:\MyPrivateKey.ppk`.

7. Highlight the public key that was generated in the textbox and copy and paste it into a new file, let's say `C:\MyPublicKey.txt`. (Do not use the **Save Public Key** button, as that adds comments and other fields that are sometimes incompatible.)

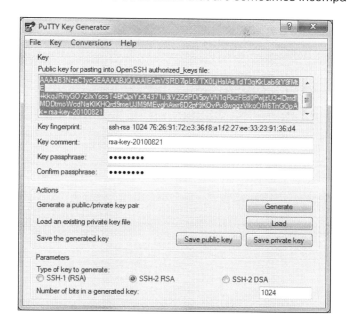

How it works...

RSA keys have become a standard for securing client/server connections for any service which chooses to take advantage of it. A client generates a key pair—a private key file and a public key file (an optional pass-phrase can be specified for enhanced security). Now, any server administrator can request that client's public key and add it to their system. The client can then securely authenticate without typing in a password.

There's more...

RSA key authentication is most often associated with SSH access, and is often referred to as SSH keys but that is misleading. RSA keys are generic and not specific to SSH. Although SSH often uses them, RSA keys can be used by any type of service that chooses to support them, such as VPN, VoIP, FTP, and so on.

See also

▶ The *Enabling the Secure Shell (SSH)* recipe
▶ The *Configuring SSH RSA key authentication* recipe

Configuring SSH RSA key authentication

This recipe describes how to configure pfSense to use an RSA key rather than a password for SSH authentication.

Getting ready

Make sure that SSH is already enabled and you have generated a public key for your client.

How to do it...

1. Browse to **System | Advanced | Secure Shell**.
2. Check **Disable password login for Secure Shell (RSA key only)**.

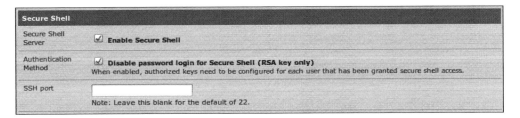

3. Edit the user we will associate with the client's public key from **System | User Manager | Edit admin**.
4. Select **Click to paste an authorized key** and paste our client's public RSA key here. When pasted, the key should appear as a single line. Be sure your text editor didn't insert any line feed characters or authentication may fail.

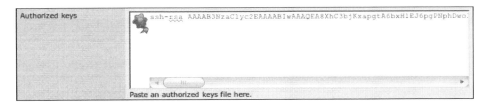

5. **Save** the changes.

How it works...

When we connect using an SSH client, we won't be asked for a password. Instead, the SSH server will use its copy of the public RSA key to send a challenge that can only be read if you posses the matching private key.

There's more...

RSA private keys can also be stored encrypted on the client machine. The SSH client will prompt for a decryption passphrase for the private key before being able to use it for authentication with the server.

See also

- ▶ The Enabling the Secure Shell (SSH) recipe
- ▶ The Generating authorized RSA keys recipe
- ▶ The Accessing the Secure Shell (SSH) recipe

Accessing the Secure Shell (SSH)

This recipe describes how to access the pfSense console from any Linux, Mac, or Windows client computer.

Getting ready

SSH must be enabled and configured on our pfSense box. Linux and Mac users will have the SSH client installed by default. Windows users will have to download and install **PuTTY**.

How to do it...

Connect via SSH from a Linux/Mac client as follows:

1. Open a terminal window and run:

   ```
   ssh admin@192.168.1.1
   ```

2. If you are using the default configuration, you'll then be prompted for a password.

3. If you are using RSA key authentication, you'll connect directly or be asked to enter the pass-phrase associated with your key. If you need to specify the location of your private key file, you can use the -i option as follows:

   ```
   ssh -i /home/matt/key/id_rsa admin@192.168.1.1
   ```

4. If you've configured pfSense to use a different port, you can specify that using the `-p` option, as in the following example:

    ```
    ssh -p 12345 admin@192.168.1.1
    ```

    Connect via SSH from a Windows client with PuTTY as follows:

5. Open PuTTY and specify your hostname or IP address.

6. Specify an alternative port if necessary (default is port 22).

7. If you are using RSA key authentication, browse to your private key file from **Connection | SSH | Auth | Private key file for authentication**.

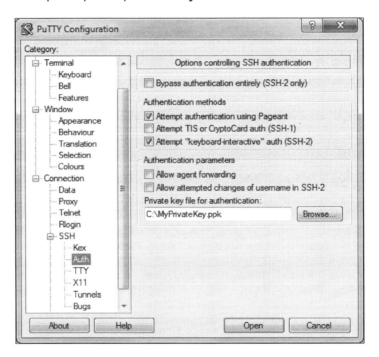

8. You'll connect and be prompted for a username.

9. You'll then be prompted for a password, or if RSA authentication is used, you'll connect directly or be prompted for your pass-phrase.

How it works...

SSH allows access to the pfSense console menu from any computer that has an SSH client. You can even access the console from your phone if you install an SSH client on your mobile device.

See also

- ▶ The *Enabling the Secure Shell (SSH)* recipe
- ▶ The *Generating authorized RSA keys* recipe
- ▶ The *Configuring SSH RSA key authentication* recipe

2

Essential Services

In this chapter, we will cover:

- ▶ Configuring the DHCP server
- ▶ Creating static DHCP mappings
- ▶ Configuring the DHCP relay
- ▶ Specifying alternate DNS servers
- ▶ Configuring the DNS forwarder
- ▶ Configuring a standalone DHCP/DNS server
- ▶ Configuring dynamic DNS

Introduction

After installing pfSense and performing the initial configuration steps, we have the basic structure of our system in place. So far, we have:

- ▶ Determined our system requirements
- ▶ Set up SSH access
- ▶ Assigned our WAN, LAN, and optional (DMZ) interfaces

At this point, we're ready to begin configuring the essential networking services that our pfSense machine will provide.

- ▶ The DHCP service allows clients to obtain IP addresses automatically
- ▶ The DNS service translates IP addresses into readable DNS names, and vice-versa
- ▶ The Dynamic DNS service allows pfSense to automatically update the dynamic DNS record when your public IP address changes

Configuring the DHCP server

This recipe describes how to configure the DHCP service in pfSense. The DHCP service assigns an IP address to any client who requests one.

Getting ready

PfSense can only be configured as a DHCP server for interfaces configured with a static IP address. Using the examples in this book, that includes the LAN and DMZ interfaces but not the WAN. This example recipe will configure the DHCP server for your DMZ interface.

How to do it...

1. Browse to **Services | DHCP Server**.
2. Choose the **DMZ** tab.
3. Check **Enable DHCP server on DMZ interface**:

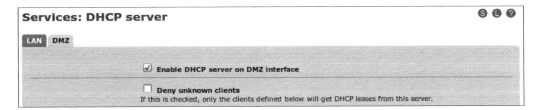

4. Choose a **Range** of IP addresses for DHCP clients to use. This range must be contiguous and within the **Available range** listed above the **Range**:

5. **Save** the changes and the DHCP service will be started.
6. **Apply** the changes, if necessary.

How it works...

A DHCP server accepts requests from clients and assigns them an available IP address.

There's more...

A DHCP server fulfills a client request by handing out the first available IP address. This means that it's very likely that a client will receive a different IP address with every request.

In order to ensure that a client always receives the same IP address, we can create static DHCP mapping. See the next recipe, *Creating static DHCP mappings*, for more information.

Deny Unknown Clients

Enabling this option ensures that only clients with static DHCP mappings will receive an IP address. DHCP requests from all other clients will be ignored.

This is different from **Enable static ARP entries** where unknown clients **will** receive an IP address, although they won't be able to communicate with the firewall (on that interface) in anyway.

DNS Servers

Specify any DNS server to be automatically assigned to our DHCP clients. If left blank, pfSense will automatically assign DNS servers to our clients in one of the following two ways:

- If DNS Forwarder is enabled, then the IP address of the interface is used. This is because the DNS Forwarder turns the pfSense machine itself into a DNS server, so the IP of the pfSense machine (that is, the gateway, which varies by interface) is assigned to each client.

- If DNS Forwarder isn't enabled, then the DNS Servers configured on the **General Setup** page are used. And of course if, **Allow DNS server list to be overridden by DHCP/PPP on WAN** is enabled in **General Setup**, then the DNS servers obtained through the WAN will be used instead.

Gateway

The interface gateway will be provided to clients by default (that is, the static IP of the interface), but can be overridden here if necessary.

Domain Name

The domain name specified in **General Setup** is used by default, but an alternative can be specified here.

Default Lease Time

An alternative lease time can be specified here for clients who do not request a specific expiration time. The default is 7200 seconds.

Maximum Lease Time

An alternative maximum lease time can be specified for clients that ask for a specific expiration time. The default is 86400 seconds.

Failover Peer IP

CARP-configured systems can specify a fail-over IP address here. See CARP configuration in the *Configuring CARP firewall failover* recipe in *Chapter 6, Redundancy, Load Balancing, and Failover* for more information.

Static ARP

Enabling static ARP entries will only allow clients with DHCP mappings to communicate with the firewall on this interface. Unknown clients will still receive an IP address, but all communication to the firewall will be blocked.

This is different from **Deny Unknown Clients** where unknown clients won't even receive an IP address.

Dynamic DNS

Enable clients to automatically register with the **Dynamic DNS** domain specified.

Additional BOOTP/DHCP Options

Enter any custom DHCP option here. Visit `http://www.iana.org/assignments/bootp-dhcp-parameters/bootp-dhcp-parameters.xml` for a list of options.

See also

  ▸ The *Creating static DHCP mappings* recipe
  ▸ The Configuring CARP firewall failover recipe in *Chapter 6, Redundancy, Load Balancing, and Failover*

Creating static DHCP mappings

This recipe describes how to add static DHCP mappings in pfSense. A static DHCP mapping ensures a client is always given the same IP address.

Getting ready

Creating static DHCP mappings is only applicable for interfaces using the DHCP service.

How to do it...

1. Browse to **Status** | **DHCP Leases** to view the list of clients who have issued DHCP requests.

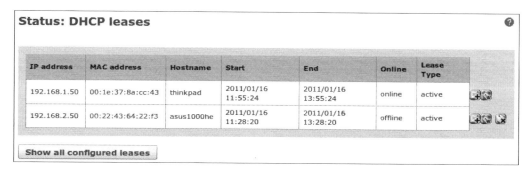

2. Click the "plus" button to add a new static DHCP mapping.
3. The MAC address will be pre-filled.
4. Enter an **IP address**, which must be outside the range of dynamically assigned DHCP addresses.
5. The **Hostname** may be pre-filled. If not, enter one.
6. Enter a **Description**.

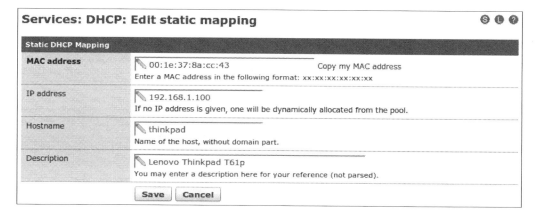

7. **Save** the changes.

8. **Apply** changes, if necessary. Scroll to the bottom of the **DHCP Server** page and verify that your new mapping exists.

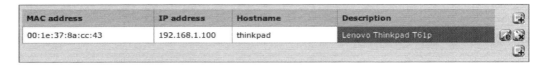

How it works...

When a client connects to our DHCP server, the firewall first checks for a mapping. If the client's MAC address matches a mapping we've specified, then the DHCP server uses the IP address specified in the mapping. If no mapping exists for our client's MAC address, our DHCP server uses an IP address from its available range.

There's more...

Static mappings can be viewed at the bottom of the DHCP Server configuration page for each interface by browsing to the **Services** | **DHCP Server** | **Interface** tab.

All static mappings for a given interface can be managed here. Existing mappings can be modified or removed, and new static mappings can be created, but you'll have to enter the MAC address manually.

See also

▶ The *Configuring the DHCP server* recipe

▶ The *Configuring the DHCP relay* recipe

Configuring the DHCP relay

This recipe describes how to configure pfSense to relay DHCP requests between broadcast domains. Specifying a DHCP relay is an alternative to configuring the DHCP service on pfSense itself.

Getting ready

DHCP Relay can only be enabled if the DHCP server is disabled on all interfaces. If necessary, first disable the DHCP service on all interfaces as follows:

1. Browse to the **Services | DHCP Server | Interface** tab (for example, LAN).
2. Uncheck **Enable DHCP Server on LAN Interface**.
3. **Save** the changes.
4. **Apply** changes, if necessary.

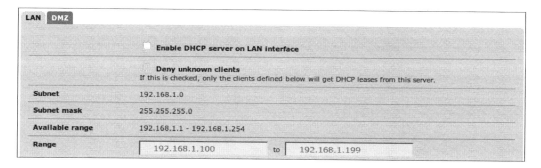

How to do it...

1. Browse to **Services | DHCP Relay**.
2. Check **Enable DHCP Relay on Interface**.
3. Select the interfaces on which the relay will be applied. Use *Ctrl* + click to select multiple interfaces.
4. Enter the IP address of the existing DHCP Servers to be used as the **Destination server**. Multiple IP addresses may be entered, separated by commas.
5. **Save** the changes.

6. **Apply** changes, if necessary.

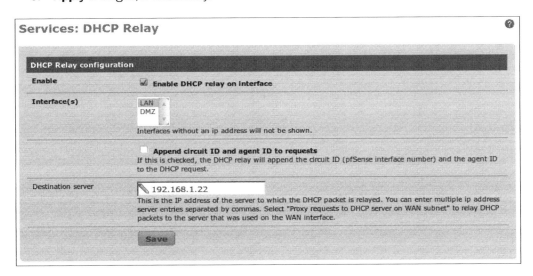

How it works...

PfSense can be configured to relay DHCP requests to existing DHCP servers. Any incoming DHCP request will be forwarded to the server(s) specified and the response will be returned to the client.

Append Circuit ID and Agent ID to Requests

PfSense can append its interface number (circuit ID) and agent ID to DHCP requests, if checked.

Relay requests to the WAN DHCP server

Select this option to relay all requests to the DHCP defined in your WAN connection.

At the time of writing this book, this feature hadn't yet been implemented in the pfSense 2.0 Beta version.

See also

- ▶ The *Configuring the DHCP server* recipe
- ▶ The *Creating static DHCP mappings* recipe

Specifying alternate DNS servers

This recipe describes how to configure pfSense to use DNS servers other than those provided by your WAN connection.

Getting ready

When it comes to resolving DNS names, most environments will rely on the DNS servers provided by their ISP through their WAN connection. By default, no DNS servers are defined in pfSense and the **Allow DNS server list to be overridden by DHCP/PPP on WAN** is checked. However, to manually specify alternate DNS servers follow the instructions in the next subsection.

How to do it...

1. Browse to **System | General Setup**.
2. The **DNS servers** section contains the following settings:
   - Specify the IP address and gateway for each of the existing **DNS servers**.
   - Uncheck **Allow DNS server list to be overridden by DHCP/PPP on WAN**.
3. **Save** changes.
4. **Apply** changes, if necessary.

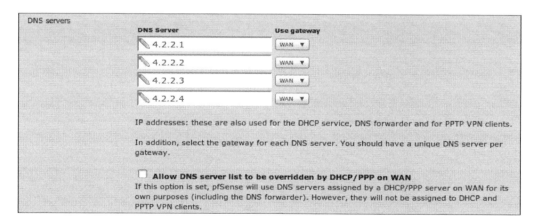

How it works...

The DNS servers specified here are the system defaults and will always take priority unless specifically overridden by the following options.

 The DNS servers listed here (4.2.2.1 – 4.2.2.4) are public DNS servers that are often very helpful when trying to troubleshoot and diagnose DNS issues.

Using the DNS Forwarder

If the DNS Forwarder is enabled, we can override the DNS servers for individual domains or even override results for individual devices. For more information, see the following *Configuring the DNS Forwarder* recipe. The DNS Forwarder takes precedence over all DNS requests.

Using your WAN DNS servers

When **Allow DNS server list to be overridden by DHCP/PPP on WAN** is enabled, pfSense will attempt to resolve DNS names using the DNS servers provided by the WAN before failing over to the servers defined in this list. After the DNS Forwarder, this option takes precedence over DNS requests.

See also

▶ The *Configuring the DNS Forwarder* recipe

Configuring the DNS Forwarder

This recipe describes how to configure the DNS Forwarder in pfSense. The DNS Forwarder allows pfSense to act as a DNS server with a variety of features.

Getting ready

The DNS Forwarder allows pfSense to resolve DNS requests using hostnames obtained by the DHCP service, static DHCP mappings, or manually entered information. The DNS Forwarder can also forward all DNS requests for a particular domain to a server specified manually.

How to do it...

1. Browse to **Services | DNS Forwarder | Enable DNS Forwarder**.
2. If **Register DHCP leases in DNS Forwarder** is enabled, any devices in **Status | DHCP Leases** will be served if a match is found.
3. If **Register DHCP static mappings in DNS Forwarder** is enabled, any devices mapped on any interface tab in **Services | DHCP Server** will be served if a match is found.

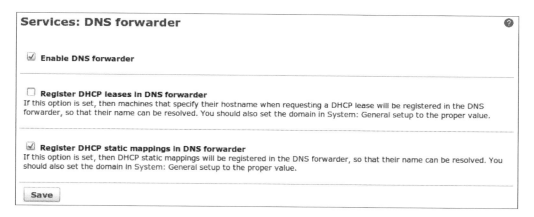

4. Specify individual **Hosts** to be served as DNS records by clicking the "plus" button to add a record. Devices in this list are checked first; so even if a record exists elsewhere, the record here takes precedence and is immediately returned.

5. Specify a DNS server for a particular **Domain** by clicking the "plus" button to add a record. These records are checked immediately after the individual records are defined above; so, a match here will take precedence over records that may exist elsewhere.

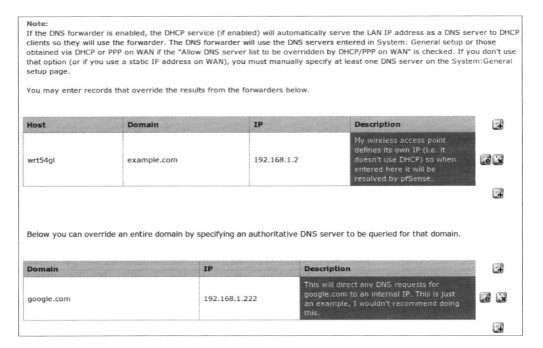

6. **Save** the changes.
7. **Apply** changes, if necessary.

How it works...

If enabled, the DNS Forwarder takes priority over all DNS requests and responds to them in the following order:

1. Individual device records (**Services | DNS Forwarder**).
2. Domain specific records (**Services | DNS Forwarder**).
3. DHCP static mappings (**Services | DHCP Server | Interface** tab).
4. DHCP leases (**Status | DHCP Leases**).

See also

▸ The *Configuring the DHCP server* recipe

▸ The *Creating static DHCP mappings* recipe

▸ The *Configuring a standalone DHCP/DNS server* recipe

Configuring a standalone DHCP/DNS server

This recipe describes how to configure pfSense as a standalone DHCP and DNS server.

How to do it...

1. Configure pfSense as a DHCP Server. See the *Configuring the DHCP server* recipe for details.

2. Create DHCP mappings for every device in the system that will obtain its IP address automatically through DHCP. See the *Creating static DHCP mappings* recipe for details.

3. Browse to **System | General Setup**.

4. Ensure that no other DNS servers are specified.

5. Enable **Allow DNS server list to be overridden by DHCP/PPP on WAN**, so that pfSense can resolve external addresses using the DNS servers provided by your ISP through your WAN connection.

6. **Save** the changes.

7. **Apply** changes, if necessary.

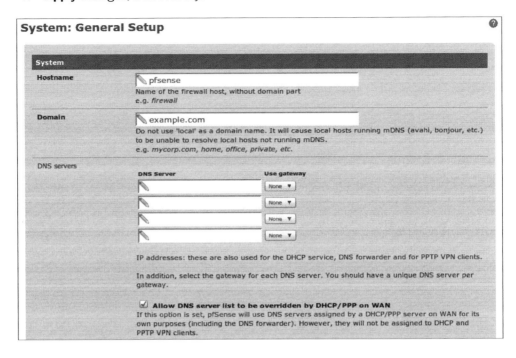

8. Browse to **System | DNS Forwarder**.
9. Check **Enable DNS Forwarder**.
10. Check **Register DHCP static mappings in DNS forwarder**.

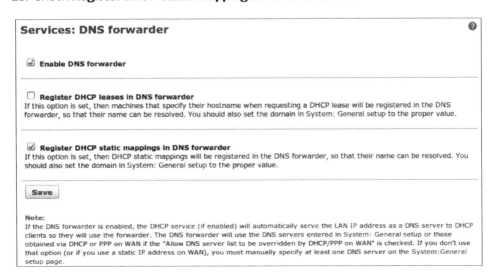

11. Create a **Host** record for any device that needs to be resolved but doesn't have a DHCP mapping (that is, devices that define their own IP).

12. Create a **Domain** record for any DNS requests you'd like to redirect for a particular domain.

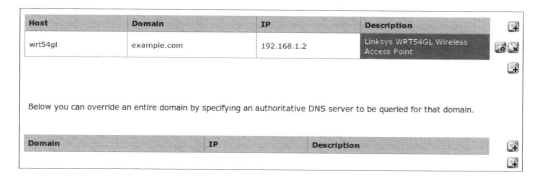

13. **Save** the changes.

14. **Apply** changes, if necessary.

How it works...

If the DNS Forwarder is enabled, every DNS request from every interface will be processed by pfSense. Individual host records are checked first, and if a match is found, the associated IP address is immediately returned.

By enabling the **Register DHCP Static Mappings** option, you won't have to worry about creating DNS records for those devices. This is my preferred method of using pfSense as a DNS server. As long as we create a static mapping for every device on our network, their hostnames will resolve automatically.

Using this method, we'll only have to add explicit hostname records for devices that specify their own IP address (that is, devices that don't use DHCP), which should be few and far between.

Register DHCP Leases in DNS Forwarder

If the **Register DHCP Leases in DNS Forwarder** option is enabled, pfSense will automatically register any devices that specify a hostname when submitting a DNS request. The downside, of course, is that not all devices submit a hostname and even when they do, it is sometimes cryptic. I prefer to only register important devices using DHCP static mappings, and all other (unimportant/unknown) devices can be referenced using their IP addresses.

See also

- ▸ The *Configuring the DHCP server* recipe
- ▸ The *Creating static DHCP mappings* recipe
- ▸ The *Configuring the DNS Forwarder* recipe

Configuring dynamic DNS

This recipe describes how to configure a dynamic DNS service in pfSense.

Getting ready

PfSense's integrated dynamic DNS service allows you to automatically update your dynamic DNS records when a change in an interface's IP address is detected.

How to do it...

1. Browse to **Services | Dynamic DNS**.
2. Click the **DynDNS** tab.
3. Click the "plus" button to add a new record.
4. Choose a **Service type** (that is, dynamic DNS service provider).
5. Specify an **Interface to monitor** (this is typically the WAN interface).
6. Specify our **Hostname** (that is, the friendly DNS name our dynamic DNS provider has supplied us with).
7. Toggle **Wildcards**, if applicable.
8. Enter your **username** and **password** you'd setup with our dynamic DNS provider.
9. Enter a friendly **description**.
10. **Save** changes.
11. **Apply** changes, if necessary.

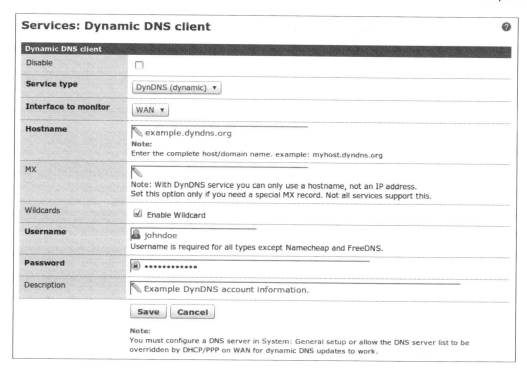

How it works...

Whenever the IP address of our interface changes, pfSense automatically connects to our dynamic DNS service and updates the IP address accordingly.

Pre-configured service types (dynamic DNS providers)

PfSense comes with the following popular dynamic DNS services pre-configured:

- DNS-O-Matic
- DynDNS (dynamic, static, custom)
- DHS
- DyNS
- easyDNS
- No-IP
- ODS
- ZoneEdit
- Loopia

- ▶ freeDNS
- ▶ DNSexit
- ▶ OpenDNS
- ▶ NameCheap

Specifying an alternative service using RFC 2136

We may specify a dynamic DNS service that doesn't come pre-configured as long as it adheres to the RFC 2136 standard. Choose the **Services | Dynamic DNS | RFC 2136** tab, and then fill in the appropriate fields using the information provided by our RFC 2136 compliant dynamic DNS service:

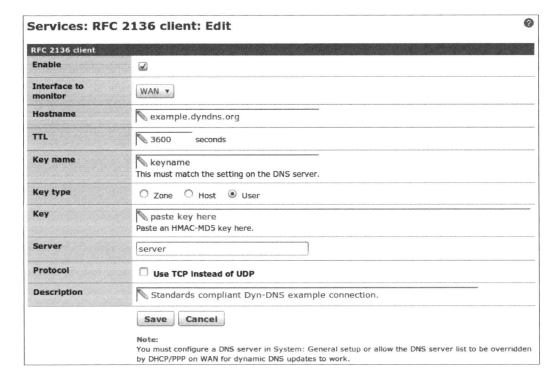

For more information, refer to:

Wikipedia – DynamicDNS

http://en.wikipedia.org/wiki/Dynamic_DNS

RFC 2136 Standard Documentation

http://tools.ietf.org/html/rfc2136

3
General Configuration

In this chapter, we will cover:

- ▶ Creating an alias
- ▶ Creating a NAT port forward rule
- ▶ Creating a firewall rule
- ▶ Creating a schedule
- ▶ Remote desktop access, a complete example

Introduction

The core functionality of any firewall involves creating port forward and firewall security rules, and pfSense is no different. These core features, plus others, can all be found on the main **Firewall** menu of the pfSense web interface.

This chapter explains how to configure these rules and the features associated with them. Once you've done a few, you'll realize just how easy it is with pfSense.

Creating an alias

This recipe describes how to use, create, edit, and delete aliases. Aliases provide a degree of separation between our rules and values that may change in the future (for example, IP addresses, ports, and so on). It's best to use aliases whenever possible.

How to do it...

1. Browse to **Firewall | Aliases**.

2. Click the "plus" button to add a new alias.

3. Add a **Name** for the alias.

4. Add an optional **Description**.

5. Select an alias **Type** and finish the configuration based on that selection.

   See the following *There's more* section for details on each alias type (Hosts, Networks, Ports, OpenVPN Users, URL, and URL Table).

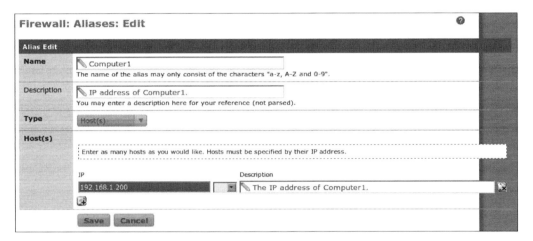

6. **Save** the changes.

7. **Apply changes**, if necessary.

How it works...

An **alias** is a place-holder (that is a variable) for information that may change. A **host alias** is a good example; we can create a host alias called **Computer1** and have it store an IP address of `192.168.1.200`.

We can then create firewall and NAT rules that use the **Computer1** alias instead of explicitly specifying the IP address of Computer1, which may change. If the IP address of Computer1 does change, then we simply edit the alias instead of modifying numerous rules.

Aliases allow for the flexibility and simplification of future changes. It's best to use aliases whenever possible.

There's more...

Adding aliases *within* aliases is a great way to manage and simplify rules. To illustrate the power of aliases, let's say our organization has a single VoIP phone that must be allowed to communicate with our VoIP server.

An example of this rule without aliases is as follows:

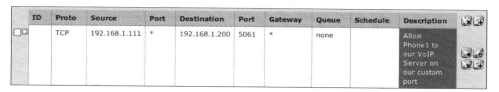

A better example, using aliases is as follows:

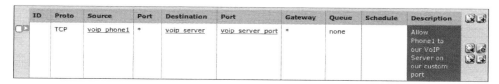

An even better example, using sub-aliases is:

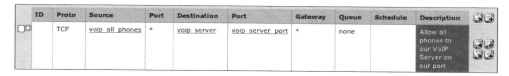

Sub-aliases will allow us to easily add more phones by simply modifying an alias:

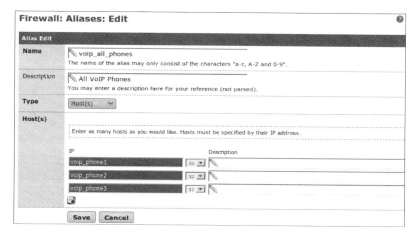

Host alias

Selecting **Host(s)** as an alias **Type** allows you to create an alias that holds one or more IP addresses:

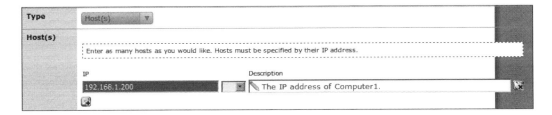

Network alias

Selecting **Network(s)** as an alias **Type** allows you to create an alias that holds one or more networks (that is ranges of IP addresses):

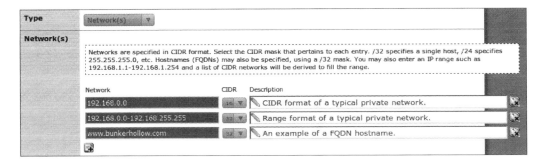

Port alias

Selecting **Port(s)** as an alias **Type** allows you to create an alias that holds one or more ports:

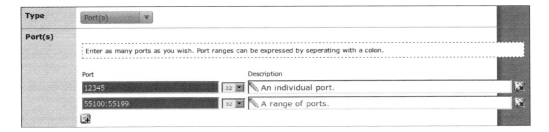

OpenVPN Users alias

Selecting **OpenVPN Users** as an alias **Type** allows you to create an alias that holds one or more OpenVPN usernames:

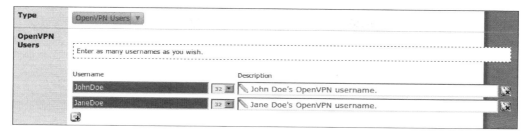

URL alias

Selecting **URL** as an alias **Type** allows you to create an alias that holds one or more URLs:

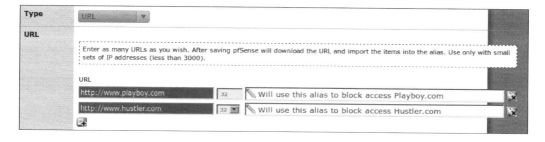

URL Table alias

Selecting **URL Table** as an alias **Type** allows you to create an alias that holds a single URL pointing to a large list of addresses. This can be especially helpful when you need to import a large list of IPs and/or subnets.

Using an alias

Aliases can be used anywhere you see a **red textbox**. Simply begin typing and pfSense will display any available aliases that match the text you've entered:

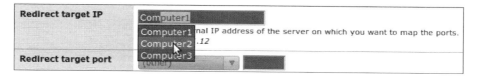

Alias auto-complete is context aware. For example, if the textbox requires a port number then pfSense will only display port alias matches.

Editing an alias

To modify an existing alias, follow these steps:

1. Browse to **Firewall** | **Aliases**.
2. Click the edit button to edit an alias.
3. Make the necessary changes.
4. **Save** the changes.
5. **Apply** the changes.

Deleting an alias:

To remove an existing alias, follow these steps:

1. Browse to **Firewall** | **Aliases**.
2. Click the delete button to delete an alias.
3. **Save** the changes.
4. **Apply** the changes.

Bulk-importing aliases

To import a list of multiple IP addresses, follow these steps:

1. Browse to **Firewall** | **Aliases**.
2. Click the import button to bulk import aliases.
3. Provide an **Alias Name**.
4. Provide an optional **Description**.
5. Paste a list of IP addresses, one per line, in the **Aliases to Import** textbox:

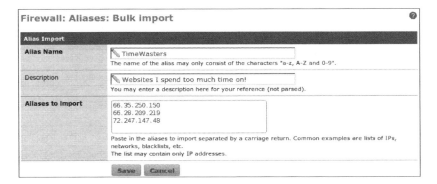

6. **Save** the changes.
7. **Apply** the changes.

See also

- ▸ The *Creating a NAT port forward rule* recipe
- ▸ The *Creating a firewall rule* recipe
- ▸ Official Documentation at `http://doc.pfsense.org/index.php/Aliases`

Creating a NAT port forward rule

This recipe describes how to create, edit, and delete port forward rules.

Getting ready

The complexity of port forward rules can vary greatly. Every aspect of a port forward rule is detailed in the following *There's More* section so for the sake of simplicity. The following is an example of a typical port forward scenario. We will create a port forward rule to forward any incoming web requests (HTTP) to a computer we've configured as a web server.

How to do it...

1. Browse to **Firewall | NAT**.
2. Select the **Port Forward** tab.
3. Click the "plus" button to create a new NAT port forward rule.
4. For **Destination port range**, choose **HTTP** for the **from** and **to** drop-down boxes.
5. For **Redirect target IP** specify the web server this traffic will be forwarded to, by alias or IP address.
6. For **Redirect target Port** choose **HTTP**.
7. Add a **Description**, such as **Forward HTTP to webserver1**.
8. **Save** the changes.

9. **Apply** the changes.

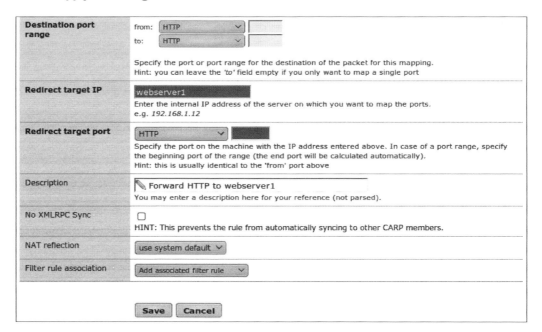

By default, a firewall rule is created to allow the forwarded traffic to pass, but it's vital to remember that NAT and firewall rules are distinct and separate. NAT rules forward traffic, while firewall rules block or allow traffic. Remember, just because a NAT rule is forwarding traffic doesn't necessarily mean the firewall rules will allow it

How it works...

All traffic passes through the list of NAT rules, with the following criteria:

- ▸ Interface
- ▸ Protocol
- ▸ Source and Source port range
- ▸ Destination and Destination port range

If any traffic matches all of this rule's criteria, that traffic will be redirected to the **Redirect target IP** and **Redirect target port** specified.

Like all rules in pfSense, NAT rules are evaluated from the top down. The first rule to match is executed immediately and the rest are skipped.

Our specific examples can be read as:

Traffic from:

- The Internet (**Interface:** WAN)
- From any client (**Source**) on any port (**Source Port Range**)

Traveling to:

- Our public IP address (**Destination** WAN address)
- With a website request (**Protocol:** TCP, **Destination Port Range:** HTTP)

Will be redirected to:

- A particular computer (**Redirect Target IP:** Webserver1)
- With the same request (**Protocol:** TCP, **Redirect Target Port:** HTTP).

There's more...

NAT rules can be configured using a variety of options, the details of each is as follows (bold items are generally the only ones which need to be modified):

- **Disabled**: Enable or disable a NAT rule by checking this box.
- **No RDR (NOT)**: Enabling this option will disable traffic redirection.
- **Interface**: Specify the interface for this NAT rule (usually WAN).
- **Protocol**: Specify the protocol for this NAT rule. Typically TCP, UDP, or TCP/UDP is specified, but GRE and ESP exist as well.
- **Source**: Typically the source is left to the default value of **any**, but you can specify a specific source if needed.
- **Source Port Range**: Generally **Source Port Range** is left to the default value of **any**, but you can specify the ports if needed.
- **Destination**: Most often, the **Destination** is left to the default value of the WAN address (that is your public IP address), but an alternative can be chosen if necessary.
- **Destination Port Range**: This is the port the traffic will be requesting. If we're forwarding web traffic, we would select **HTTP**, which is so common that it's built into the drop-down list, but choosing **(other)** and specifying port 80 would work just the same. If specifying a custom port (let's say we want to forward torrent traffic on port 46635), remember to **use an alias**!

▶ **Redirect Target IP**: This is the IP address of the internal computer we will forward traffic to. Remember to **use an alias**!

▶ **Redirect Target Port**: This is the port of the computer specified previously that traffic will be forwarded to. Remember to **use an alias**!

▶ **Description**: The description provided here will be copied into any firewall rules (and preceded by the word "NAT") that are automatically generated.

▶ **No XMLRPC Sync**: Enable this option to prevent this rule from being applied to any redundant firewalls using CARP. Refer to the Configuring CARP Firewall Failover section in *Chapter 6, Redundancy, Load Balancing, and Failover* for more information.

▶ **NAT Reflection**: Using system default is almost always the case, but **NAT Reflection** can be enabled or disabled as per rule, if needed.

▶ **Filter Rule Association**: A firewall rule will automatically be created and associated to this NAT rule.

Port redirection

A true port forwarding rule will pass traffic to an internal machine on the *same* port that was requested (that is, the **Destination port range** and **Redirect target port** will match). However, there's nothing stopping you from redirecting to a different port if you'd like. There are two typical reasons for doing so:

▶ **Security Through Obscurity**: Everyone knows that the standard HTTP port is 80, but suppose you have a "secret" website which you don't want to be accessed easily. You can set the **Destination Port Range** to some obscure port (for example, 54321) and forward that to your internal web server's standard HTTP port 80. Users will have to know to browse to `http://www.example.com:54321` in order to access it.

▶ **Single Public IP Address**: Smaller environments with only a single public IP address may find themselves stuck if they want to expose a lot of public services. For example, "I want to remote into 2 different machines, but I only have 1 public IP address." With port redirection, we'll create two different NAT rules. The first will redirect port 50001 to Computer1 on MSRDP (port 3389) and the second will redirect port 50002 to Computer2 on MSRDP (port 3389). You can then remote into different machines using a single IP by specifying particular ports (for example, example.com:50001, example.com:50002, and so on).

See also

▶ The *Creating an alias* recipe

▶ The *Creating a firewall rule* recipe

▶ The *Configuring CARP firewall failover* recipe in *Chapter 6, Redundancy, Load Balancing, and Failover*

Creating a firewall rule

This recipe describes how to create a firewall rule.

Getting ready

As an example, we will create a firewall rule to allow the web traffic forwarded in by the NAT port forward rule we created in the previous recipe. If you've been following along, you'll know that the previous recipe automatically created the firewall rule we need, but instead we could have specified **None** for **Filter Rule Association** and used this recipe to create the rule ourselves.

How to do it...

1. Browse to **Firewall | Rules**.
2. Select the **WAN** tab.
3. Click the "plus" button to create a new firewall rule.
4. Specify the **WAN Interface**.
5. Specify the **TCP Protocol**.
6. Specify **any** as the **Source**.
7. Specify **any** as the **Source Port Range**.
8. Specify **Webserver1** as our **Destination**.
9. Specify **HTTP** as our **Destination Port Range**.
10. Specify a **Description**.
11. **Save** the changes.

12. **Apply** changes.

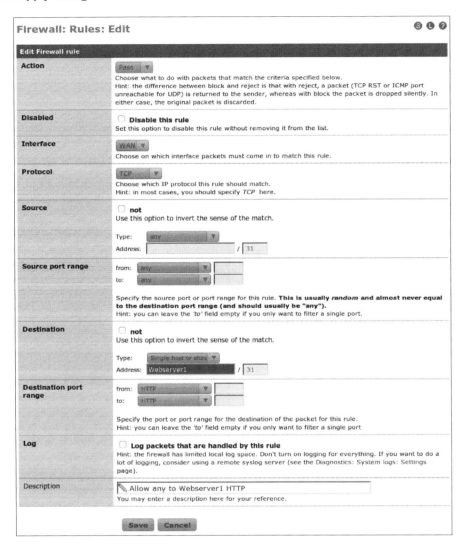

How it works...

All traffic passes through the list of firewall rules. If any traffic packet matches all of the rules' criteria, that rule we be executed (the packet will be allowed or denied).

Like all rules in pfSense, firewall rules are evaluated from the top down. The first rule to match is executed immediately and the rest are skipped. See the following *Ordering Firewall Rules* section for more information.

This rule can be read as: "Any port from any client on the Internet is allowed to access our web server's port 80".

There's more...

Firewall rules are highly configurable. Details of each firewall rule option are as follows:

- ▶ **Action**: The type of action defined will be enforced if the rule is matched.
    - ❏ **Pass**: If all the criteria match, the packet will be allowed to pass.
    - ❏ **Block**: If all the criteria matches, the packet will not be allowed to pass (some refer to this as a **silent drop**).
    - ❏ **Reject**: If all the criteria match, the packet will be returned to the sender.
- ▶ **Disabled**: Disable a rule without having to delete it entirely.
- ▶ **Interface**: Traffic originating from the specified interface will be subject to this rule. This is typically the WAN.
- ▶ **Protocol**: Specify the protocol to be matched; this varies depending on the type of traffic this rule defines.
- ▶ **Source**: This is typically **any** when referring to incoming traffic.
- ▶ **Source Port Range**: This is typically **any** when referring to incoming traffic.
- ▶ **Destination**: This is typically the alias or IP address of computer which is servicing this traffic.
- ▶ **Destination Port Range**: This is typically the specific port of the computer which is servicing this traffic.
- ▶ **Log**: Enable logging to record packets that match this rule.
- ▶ **Description**: Enter meaningful descriptions that will make it easier to understand the rule.

We rarely know the source port!

When specifying rules, it's important to remember that the **Source Port Range** is almost always set to **any**. People often make the mistake of specifying a **Source Port Range** when they shouldn't. Remember, when you request a website, you are requesting port 80 on someone else's computer and your computer decides what port to open on yours. This is your source port, an ever-changing port which you probably never know about. So 99 percent of the time, we won't know the **Source Port Range** of the traffic we are allowing in.

Ordering firewall rules

PfSense rules are always evaluated from the top down. The first rule to match is executed and the rest of the rules are skipped. Many administrators will include very specific rules at the top and more generic rules at the bottom. To reorder a rule, select the rule and then click the appropriate **move selected rules before this rule** button:

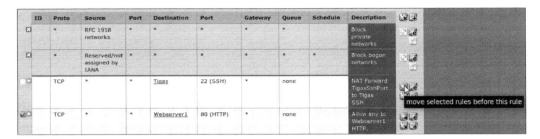

Duplicating a firewall rule

Often, we may want to create a new rule that's very similar to an existing rule. To save time, we can create a new rule that's pre-filled with the same options as an existing rule by clicking the "plus" button:

Advanced features

New to pfSense 2.0 is the firewall rule **Advanced Features** section. Each of the following features can be specified as criteria for a rule. If an advanced feature is specified, the rule will only be executed if a match is found. Click the **Advanced** button to display the following configuration settings for each feature:

 ▸ **Source OS**: This option will attempt to match the operating system of the source traffic:

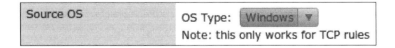

 ▸ **Diffserv Code Point**: **Diffserv** is a mechanism for providing Quality of Service (QoS) of network traffic. Systems can prioritize traffic based on their code point values:

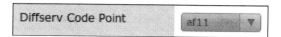

▶ **Advanced Options**: Allows for the specification of advanced IP Options:

Advanced Options	
	☐
	This allows packets with IP options to pass. Otherwise they are blocked by default. This is usually only seen with multicast traffic.
	☐
	This will disable auto generated reply-to for this rule.
	[_____]
	You can mark a packet matching this rule and use this mark to match on other NAT/filter rules. It is called **Policy filtering**
	[_____]
	You can match packet on a mark placed before on another rule.
	[_____]
	Maximum state entries this rule can create
	[_____]
	Maximum number of unique source hosts
	[_____]
	Maximum number of established connections per host
	[_____]
	Maximum state entries per host
	[_____] / [____▼]
	Maximum new connections / per second(s)
	[_____]
	State Timeout in seconds
	NOTE: Leave fields blank to disable that feature.

▶ **TCP Flags**: Specific TCP flags may be set here:

TCP flags		FIN	SYN	RST	PSH	ACK	URG
	set	☐	☐	☐	☐	☐	☐
	out of	☐	☐	☐	☐	☐	☐
	☐ **Any flags.**						
	Use this to choose TCP flags that mustbe set or cleared for this rule to match.						

- ▶ **State Type**: Specify a particular state tracking mechanism:

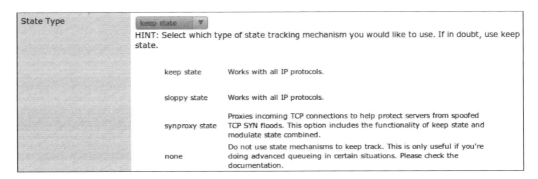

- ▶ **No XMLRPC Sync**: Prevent a rule from syncing with the other CARP members:

- ▶ **Schedule**: Specify the schedule for when this rule is valid. Schedules defined in **Firewall | Schedules** will appear here:

- ▶ **Gateway**: Gateways other than the default may be specified here:

- ▶ **In/Out**: Specify alternative queues and virtual interfaces:

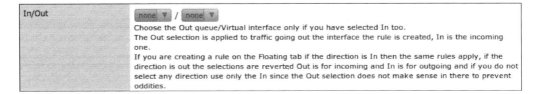

- ▶ **Ackqueue/Queue**: Specify alternative acknowledge queues:

Choose the Acknowledge Queue only if you have selected Queue.

▶ **Layer7**: Specify an alternative **Layer7** container:

Choose a Layer7 container to apply application protocol inspection rules. These are valid for TCP and UDP protocols only.

See also

▶ The *Creating an alias* recipe
▶ The *Creating a NAT port forward rule* recipe
▶ The *Creating a schedule* recipe

Creating a schedule

This recipe describes how to create a schedule.

Getting ready

Schedules allow us to specify *when* rules are enabled. They are primarily used with firewall rules, but their generic design allows them to be used with other existing and future pfSense features. If a firewall rule specifies a schedule, the rule is only enabled during that time period. In the following example, we'll define a schedule for our normal 9am-5pm work hours.

 When creating schedules, it's essential to have your NTP time-sync settings properly configured against a reliable server. Also be aware of time-zone differences and day-light savings time.

How to do it...

1. Browse to **Firewall | Schedules**.
2. Click the "plus" button to create a new schedule.
3. Enter a **Schedule Name**, such as **WorkHours**.
4. Enter a **Description**, such as **Regular work week hours**.
5. In the **Month** section, click **Mon**, **Tue**, **Wed**, **Thu**, and **Fri** to select all the days of the work week.

6. Specify a 9 am as the **Start Time** and 5 pm as the **Stop Time**.

7. Enter a T**ime Range Description**, such as **Monday-Friday 9am-5pm**.

8. Click **Add Time**.

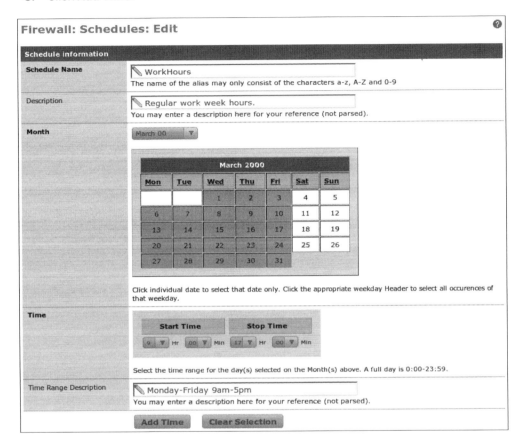

9. Note that the repeating time is added to **Configured Ranges**:

10. **Save** the changes.

11. **Apply** the changes, if necessary.

How it works...

Features associated with a schedule will only be valid during the schedule specified. To associate a firewall rule with the schedule we've just created:

1. Edit an existing firewall rule, or create a new one.
2. Click the **Schedule Advanced** button to show the scheduling options.
3. Choose **WorkHours** as our **Schedule**:

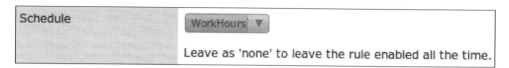

4. Save the changes.
5. Apply the changes.

There's more...

Icons exist throughout the system to help determine at a glance if a schedule is active or not:

▶ **Firewall | Schedules**: Active schedules show a "clock" icon:

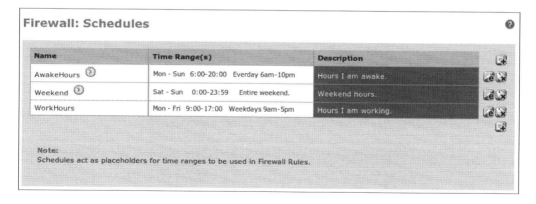

> ▶ **Firewall | Rules**: Rules with active schedules (meaning the rules which are enabled) show a "green arrow" in the schedule column.

> Rules with inactive schedules (meaning the rules which are disabled) show a "red x" in the schedule column:

ID	Proto	Source	Port	Destination	Port	Gateway	Queue	Schedule	Description	
☒	*	RFC 1918 networks	*	*	*	*	*		Block private networks	
☒	*	Reserved/not assigned by IANA	*	*	*	*	*	*	Block bogon networks	
☐▷	TCP	*	*	Webserver1	80 (HTTP)	*	none	☒ WorkHours	Allow any to Webserver1 HTTP during work hours.	
☐▷	TCP	*	*	Webserver1	80 (HTTP)	*	none	☐ Weekend	Allow any to Webserver1 HTTP on the weekend.	

Selecting days or days of the week

The **Month** section works in two ways:

> ▶ **Selecting specific days**: Switch to the correct month and click the specific day (the year is irrelevant; any days selected will repeat every year):

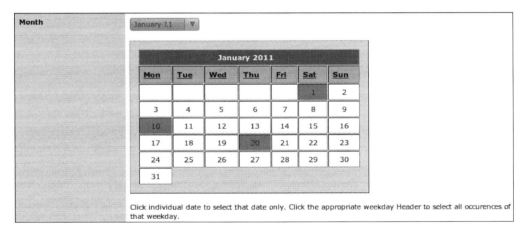

> ▶ **Selecting days of the week**: Click the day of the week heading link (the month is irrelevant, the day of the week will always repeat):

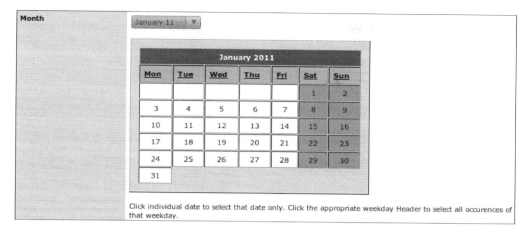

Click individual date to select that date only. Click the appropriate weekday Header to select all occurences of that weekday.

See also

▸ The *Creating an alias* recipe

▸ The *Creating a NAT port forward rule* recipe

▸ The *Creating a firewall rule* recipe

Remote desktop access, a complete example

The recipe describes how to access an internal machine using Microsoft's Remote Desktop Protocol (RDP).

Getting ready

The purpose of this recipe is to demonstrate a typical firewall task from start to finish. The following example will demonstrate how to remote into an internal machine from anywhere on the Internet. Doing so requires the configuration of the following features, which have all been covered in recipes preceding this point in the book:

▸ DHCP Server

▸ DHCP static mappings

▸ DNS Forwarder

▸ Aliases

▸ NAT port forwarding

▸ Firewall rules

• Schedules

How to do it...

1. Let's connect a computer to our network.

2. Browse to **Status | DHCP Leases** to find the newly added computer. Click the "plus" button to assign a new static mapping for the device:

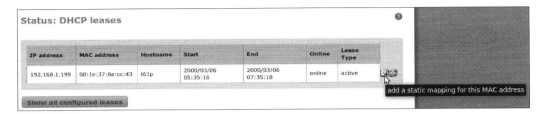

3. Let's assign it a static IP address of **192.168.1.200** and call it **laptop1**:

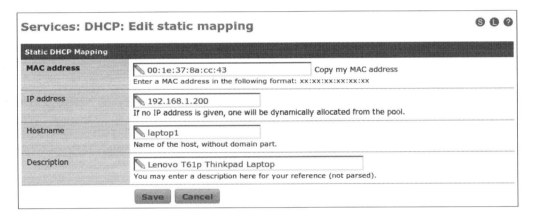

4. Let's make sure our DNS Forwarder is configured to automatically serve static mappings at **Services | DNS Forwarder**, so that we can easily reference our laptop computer by name:

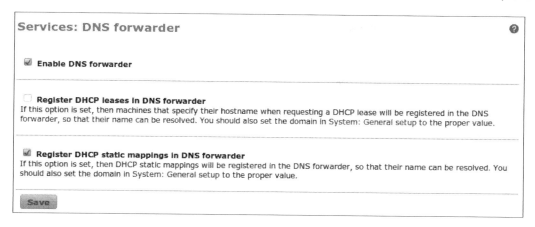

5. Let's create an alias to be used when referencing this machine within pfSense from **Firewall | Aliases**:

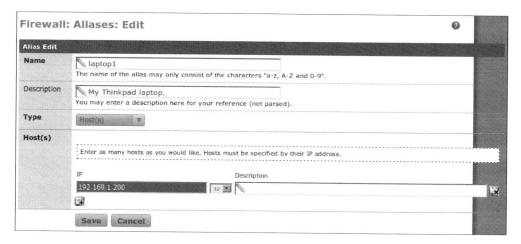

6. Let's create a schedule at **Firewall | Schedules** so that remote access is only enabled while we're at work, since that's when we intend to use it. Also, we can rest a little easier that it's not susceptible to attack while we're sleeping:

Name	Time Range(s)		Description
WorkHours	Mon - Fri	9:00-17:00	Regular work week hours.

7. Let's create a NAT rule to forward all remote desktop (RDP) requests to our laptop from **Firewall | NAT**. From researching on "remote desktop protocol" on the Internet, we know we are dealing with TCP port 3389 (PfSense includes a predefined MS RDP port because it's so common):

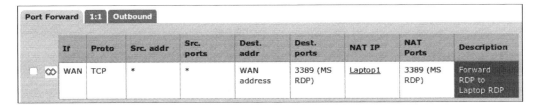

8. Next, we need to add our schedule to the firewall rule that was automatically created from **Firewall | Rules**:

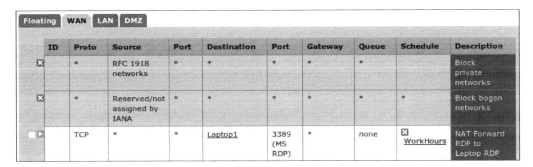

9. **Save** all changes.
10. **Apply** all changes, if necessary.

How it works...

Our NAT rule forwards all RDP requests to our laptop. The NAT rule is always enabled. Our firewall rule allows anyone to remote into our laptop, but only during work hours (Monday-Friday, 9am-5pm). At the time of writing this book, it's Sunday at 4 pm; so you can see the rule is correctly disabled.

There's more...

If we really wanted to tighten security, we could restrict external access to only our IP address at work. We would first create an alias for our office's IP address:

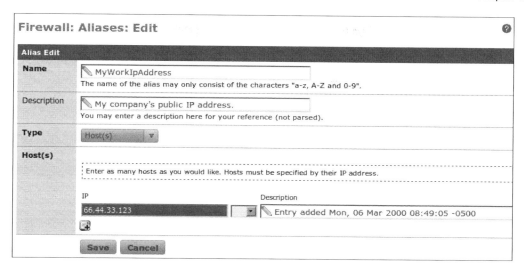

Then we would modify our firewall rule to only apply to requests coming from our company's IP address (remember, traffic that doesn't match any rules is blocked by default). Now, with pfSense's Filter Rule Association, we won't be able to modify the **Source** of our firewall rule directly.

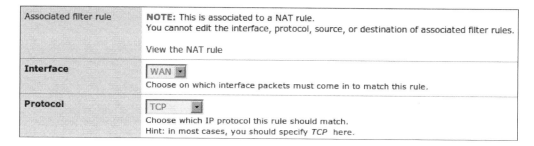

So, we'll modify the NAT rule instead. From Source, click the **Advanced** option and specify the alias for our company's public IP address.

Then we'll double check if those changes have propagated down to our firewall rule, which they have:

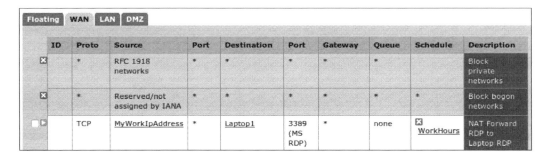

See also

▶ The *Configuring DHCP servers* recipe in *Chapter 2, Essential Services*

▶ The *Creating static DHCP mappings* recipe in *Chapter 2, Essential Services*

▶ The *Configuring dynamic DNS* recipe in *Chapter 2, Essential Services*

▶ The *Creating an alias* recipe

▶ The *Creating a NAT* port *forward rule* recipe

▶ The *Creating a firewall rule* recipe

▶ The *Creating a schedule* recipe

4
Virtual Private Networking

In this chapter, we will cover:

- ▸ Creating an IPsec VPN tunnel
- ▸ Configuring the L2TP VPN service
- ▸ Configuring the OpenVPN service
- ▸ Configuring the PPTP VPN service

Introduction

Virtual Private Networking (**VPN**) is a cornerstone of modern computer systems. A VPN connection allows a remote user to securely connect to a network and access resources as if he were connected locally.

Like all great things, there are a variety of VPN services out there and pfSense has four most popular implementations built right in. **OpenVPN** is emerging as the standard VPN protocol, but be aware that you'll have to download client software for any Microsoft machine (OpenVPN support isn't built into Windows). IPSec is more complex, but is also a very popular VPN implementation. PPTP and L2TP services are frequently getting replaced with the aforementioned alternatives, but their use is still widespread and everything you need to create a connection is built into most major operating systems.

This chapter describes how to configure pfSense to serve any or all of the four major VPN implementations—IPSec, L2TP, OpenVPN, and PPTP.

Creating an IPsec VPN tunnel

This recipe describes how to configure pfSense to establish a VPN link using an IPsec tunnel.

Getting ready

IPSec is often the preferred method for network-to-network (as opposed to client-to-network) connections. A typical scenario involves creating a permanent, secure connection between headquarters and a branch office.

 Networks connected through VPN must use different subnets. For example, if both networks use the 192.168.1.0/24 subnet, then VPN will not work.

How to do it...

1. Browse to **VPN | Ipsec**.
2. Click the "plus" button to create an IPsec tunnel.
3. Specify the **Remote gateway**.
4. Add a **Description**:

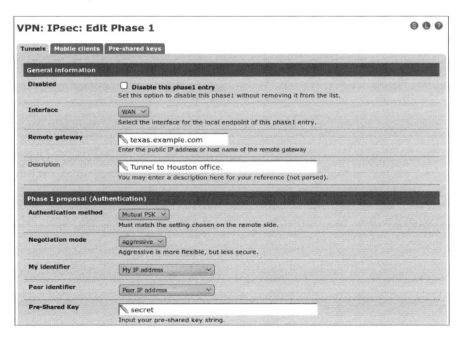

5. Enter a **Pre-Shared Key**.

6. **Save** the changes.

7. Check **Enable IPsec**.

8. **Save** the changes:

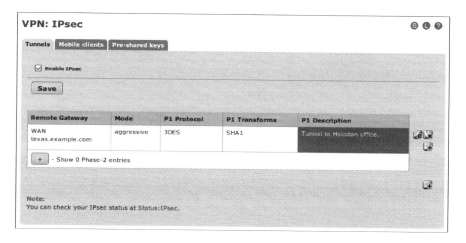

9. **Apply** changes, if necessary.

10. Browse to **Firewall | Rules**.

11. Select the **IPsec** tab.

12. Click the "plus" button to add a new firewall rule.

13. Set **Destination** to the LAN subnet.

14. Set **Destination port** to **any**.

15. Add a **description**, such as **Allow IPsec traffic to LAN**.

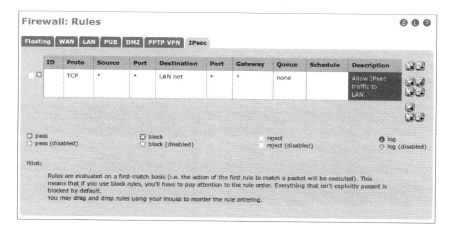

16. **Save** the changes.

17. **Apply** changes, if necessary.

How it works...

Once an IPsec tunnel is established, clients connected to either network will have access to each other as if they were connected on different subnets of the same physical network.

See also

▸ The *Configuring the L2TP VPN service* recipe

▸ The *Configuring the OpenVPN service* recipe

▸ The *Configuring the PPTP VPN service* recipe

Configuring the L2TP VPN service

This recipe describes how to set up pfSense as a L2TP VPN server.

Getting ready

It's important to understand that unlike the other VPN implementations, L2TP does *not* encrypt any data. L2TP is simply a method of encapsulation and should only be used over trusted networks, or in conjunction with IPsec. A major advantage of L2TP, however, is that it can be used with non-IP networks.

 Networks connected through VPN must use different subnets. For example, if both networks use the 192.168.1.0/24 subnet, then VPN will not work.

How to do it...

1. Browse to **VPN | L2TP**.

2. On the **Configuration** tab, check **Enable L2TP Server**.

3. Specify an unused IP for the **Server address**.

4. Specify an unused starting IP for the **Remote address range**. The range will be as long as the number of users specified in step 6.

5. Specify a **Subnet mask**.

6. Specify **Number of L2TP users**:

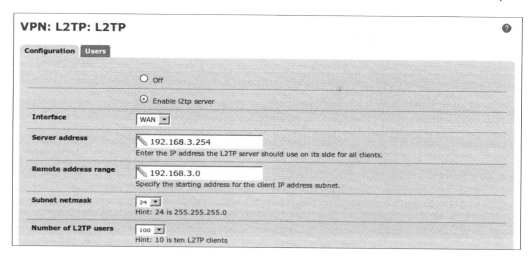

7. **Save** the changes.

8. Click the **Users** tab.

9. Click the "plus" button to create a new user.

10. Specify a **username** and **password**:

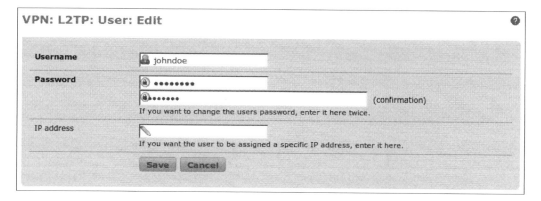

11. Save the changes:

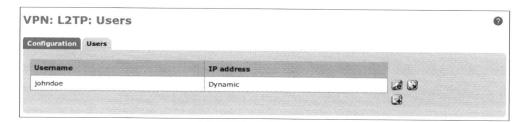

12. Browse to **Firewall | Rules**.

13. Select the **L2TP VPN** tab.

14. Click the "plus" button to create a new firewall rule.

15. Set the **Destination** to the LAN subnet.

16. Set the **Destination port range** to **any**.

17. Enter a **Description**, such as **Allow L2TP Clients to LAN**.

18. **Save** the changes:

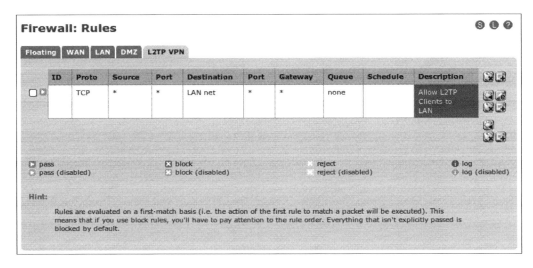

19. **Apply** changes, if necessary.

How it works...

The L2TP service allows external users to remotely access a network interface of our choice. Users connected to our network using an L2TP VPN client will have access to the network as if they were on physically connected clients.

Connecting from a Windows 7 client

To create a L2TP VPN connection from a Windows 7 machine:

1. Open **Control Panel | Network and Internet | View network status and tasks** (opens Network and Sharing Center):

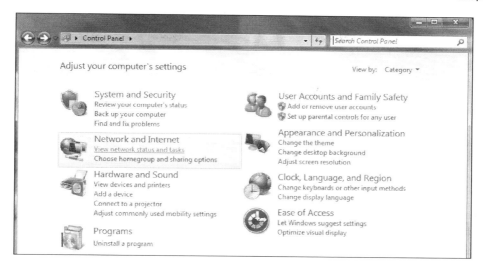

2. Click **Set up a new connection or network**:

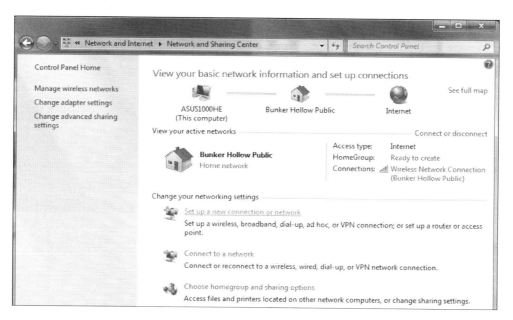

3. Choose **Connect to a workplace** (dial-up or VPN connection):

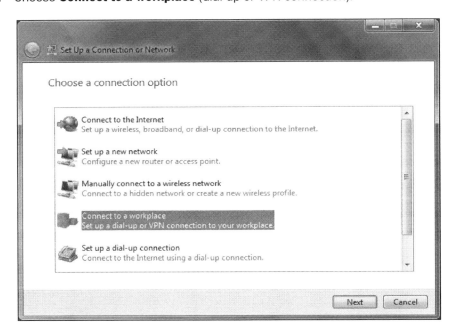

4. Choose **Use my Internet connection (VPN)**:

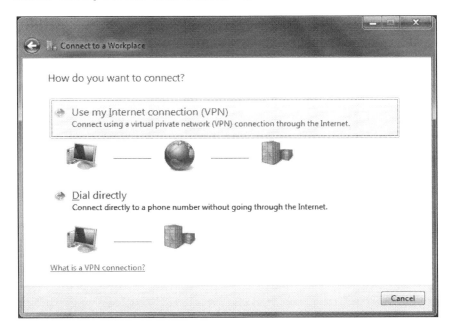

5. Enter the **Server Address** we configured for the network we're connecting to. (If the L2TP server address you configured isn't directly accessible, you will have to NAT port-forward L2TP traffic).

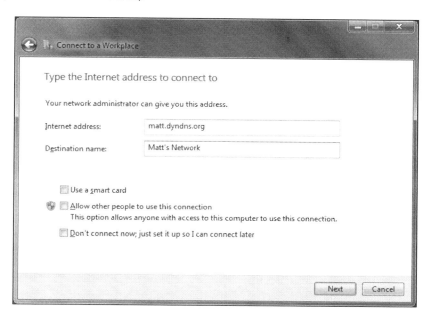

6. Enter the **username** and **password** if any:

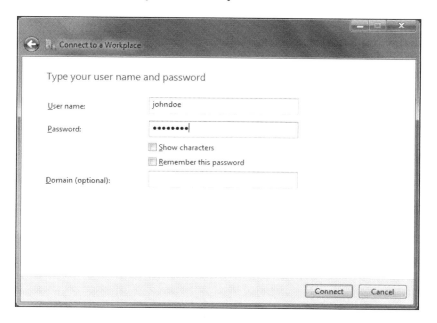

7. **Connect!** Windows will automatically detect whether the server is accepting L2TP or PPTP connections and configure itself accordingly.

See also

▶ The *Creating a NAT port forward rule* recipe in *Chapter 3, General Configuration*

▶ The *Creating an IPsec VPN tunnel* recipe

▶ The *Configuring the OpenVPN service* recipe

▶ The *Configuring the PPTP VPN service* recipe

Configuring the OpenVPN service

This recipe describes how to configure pfSense to accept OpenVPN connections.

How to do it...

1. Browse to **VPN | OpenVPN**.
2. Click the **Wizards** tab.
3. Select **Local User Access** for **Type of Server**:

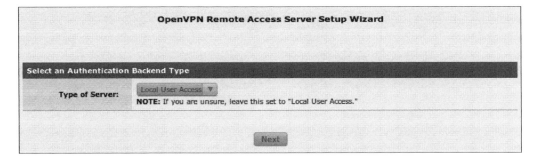

4. Click **Next**.
5. Enter a **Descriptive name** such as **MyCaCert** for the new CA certificate.
6. Enter **US** for **Country Code**.
7. Enter a **State or Province**, such as **New York**.
8. Enter a **City**, such as **New York**.
9. Enter an **Organization**, such as **Blue Key Consulting**.
10. Enter an **E-mail** address, such as **contact@example.com**.
11. Click the **Add new CA** button:

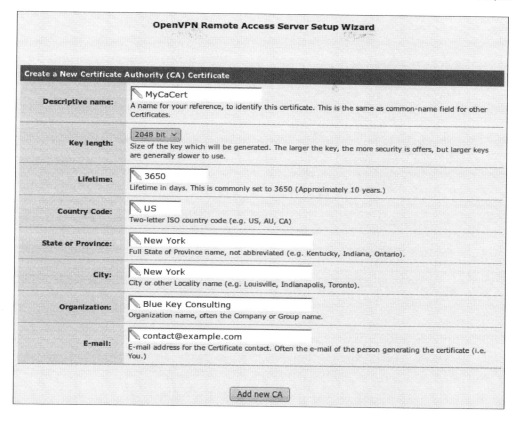

12. Enter a **Descriptive name** for the new Server certificate, **MyServerCert**. Creating a server certificate will look almost identical to the CA certificate you created in the previous step.

13. Enter **US** for **Country Code**.

14. Enter a **State or Province**, such as **New York**.

15. Enter a **City**, such as **New York**.

16. Enter an **Organization**, such as **Blue Key Consulting**.

17. Enter an **E-mail** address, such as **contact@example.com**.

18. Click the **Create new Certificate** button:

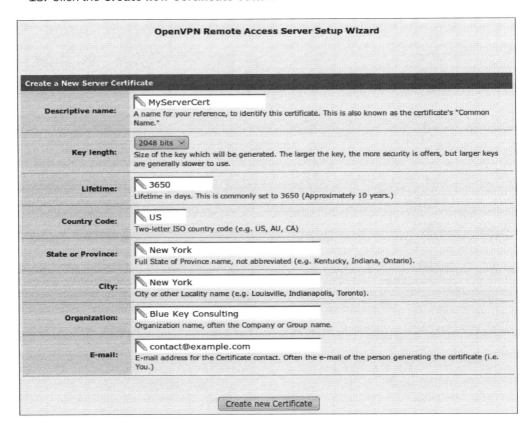

19. Specify a **description**, such as **My OpenVPN Connection**:

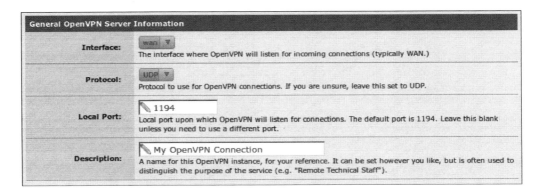

20. Specify a **Tunnel Network** in CIDR notation. This should be an unused interface range (that, of course, doesn't overlap with the existing LAN) such as **192.168.4.0/24**.

21. Specify the **Local Network**, in CIDR notation that clients will be able to access. This is generally our LAN network, **192.168.1.0/24**.

22. Specify a maximum number of **Concurrent Connections**:

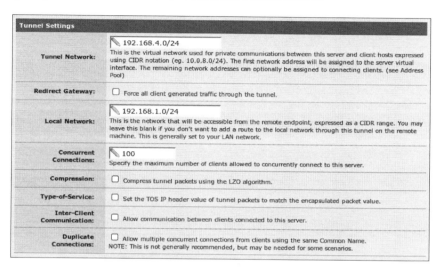

23. Click the **Next** button.

24. Check **Add a rule to permit traffic from clients on the Internet to the OpenVPN server process**.

25. Check **Add a rule to allow all traffic from connected clients to pass across the VPN tunnel**:

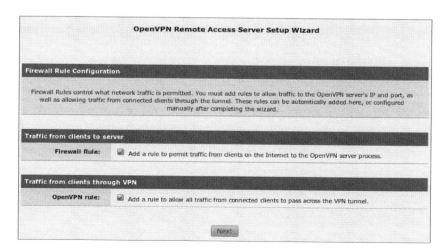

26. Click **Next**:

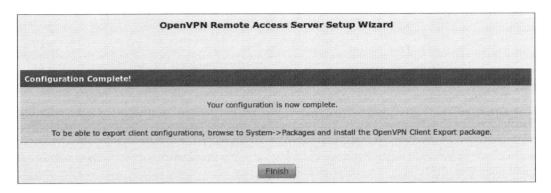

27. Click on **Finish**:

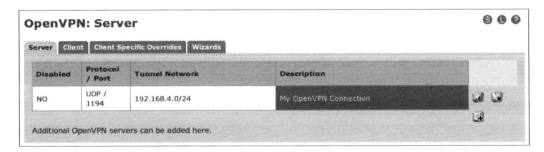

How it works...

The OpenVPN service allows external users to establish a secure, encrypted connection to our network. Users will connect to the network using an OpenVPN client and once authenticated, the user will have access to the network as if they were physically connected.

Encryption algorithms

Choosing the correct encryption algorithm for your hardware is critical for maximum hardware performance. Many VPN expansion cards, such as those found on Netgate systems using Alix boards require AES-128-CBC. Check with your hardware vendor for details.

OpenVPN Client Export

There is a pfSense package called the **OpenVPN Client Export Utility** that simplifies the client configuration process. To install it:

1. Browse to **System | Packages**.
2. Click the **Available Packages** tab.
3. Locate the **OpenVPN Client Export Utility** and click the "plus" button to begin installation:

4. The package will be downloaded and installed automatically.

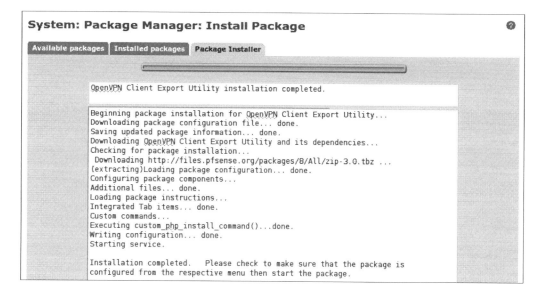

5. The plugin will be installed to the **VPN | OpenVPN** menu.

See also

▸ The *Creating an IPsec VPN tunnel* recipe

▸ The *Configuring the L2TP VPN service* recipe

▸ The *Configuring the PPTP VPN service* recipe

Configuring the PPTP VPN service

This recipe describes how to configure pfSense to accept PPTP VPN connections.

How to do it...

1. Browse to the **VPN | PPTP | Configuration** tab.
2. Check **Enable PPTP server**.
3. Choose **No. PPTP users**.
4. Enter an unused IP address to specify as the PPTP **Server address**. PfSense's PPTP service will listen on this address.
5. Enter the start of the **Remote address range** for clients that connect. Remember, a valid range must be large enough for the number of users specified above.

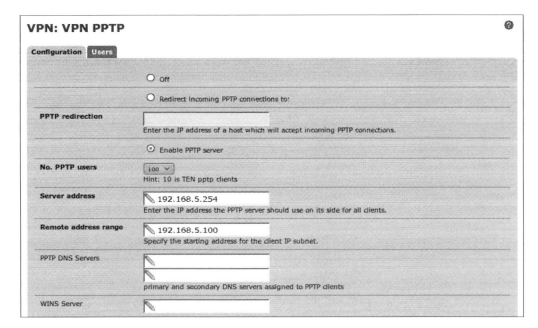

6. Check **Require 128-bit encryption**:

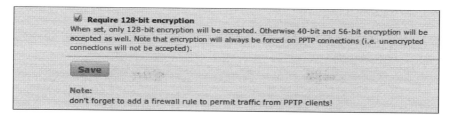

7. **Save** the changes.

8. Select the **Users** tab.

9. Click the "plus" button to add a user.

10. Specify **Username** and **Password**.

11. **Save** the changes:

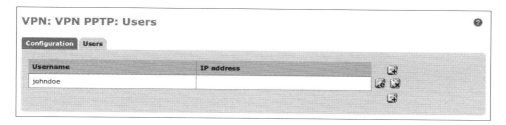

12. Browse to **Firewall | Rules**.

13. Select the **PPTP VPN** tab.

14. Click the "plus" button to create a new firewall rule.

15. Set the **Destination** to LAN subnet.

16. Set the **Destination port range** to **any**.

17. Enter a **Description**, such as **Allow PPTP Clients to LAN**.

18. **Save** the changes:

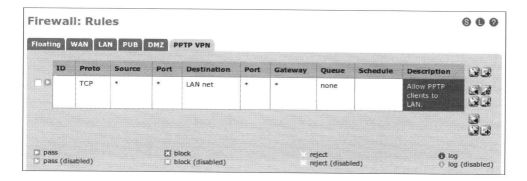

19. Apply changes, if necessary.

How it works...

The PPTP service allows external users to establish a secure, encrypted connection to our network. Users will connect to the network using a PPTP client and, once authenticated, the user will have access to the network as if they were physically connected.

Connecting from a Windows 7 client

Perform the following steps to create a PPTP VPN connection from a Windows 7 machine:

1. Open **Control Panel | Network and Internet | View network status and tasks** (opens Network and Sharing Center):

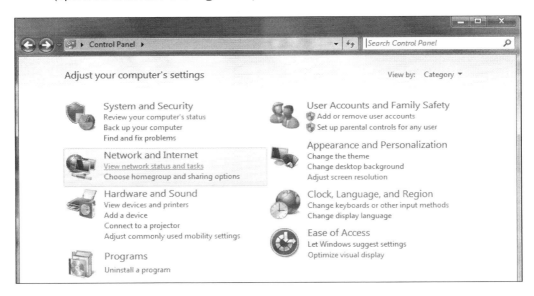

2. Click **Set up a new connection or network**:

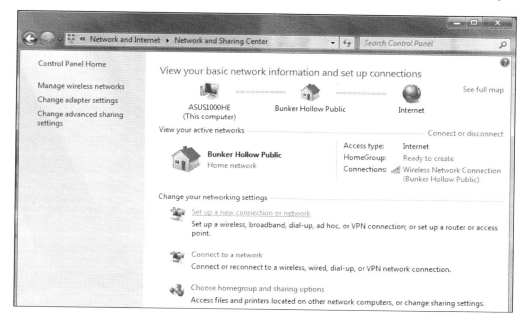

3. Choose **Connect to a workplace** (dial-up or VPN connection):

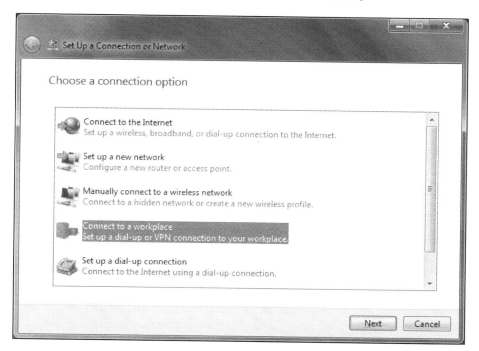

4. Choose **Use my Internet connection (VPN)**:

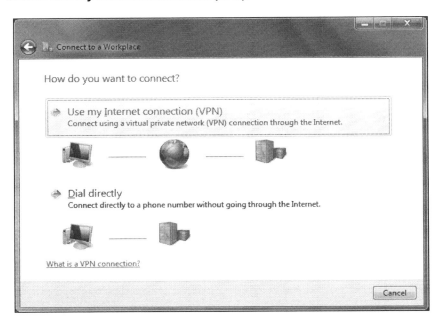

5. Enter the public IP address or hostname of the network we're connecting to:

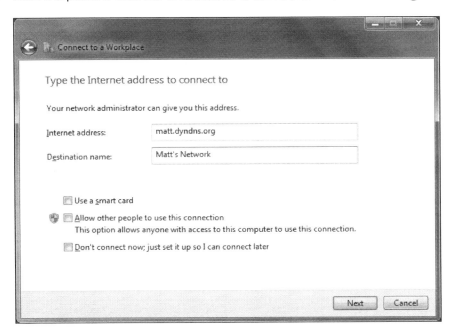

6. Enter the **User name** and **Password** you've configured:

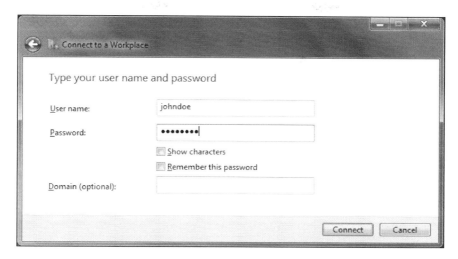

7. Click on **Connect**! Windows will automatically detect whether the server is accepting PPTP or L2TP connections and configure itself accordingly.

Connecting from a Ubuntu 10.10 client

Perform the following steps to create a PPTP VPN connection from a Ubuntu machine:

1. Open **System | Preferences | Network Connections**.

2. Choose **VPN** tab | **Add** button to create a new VPN connection.

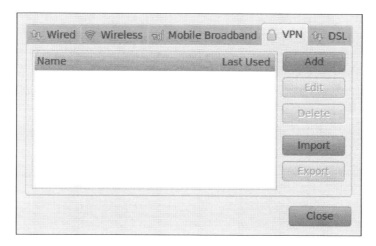

3. Select **PPTP** and click the **Create...** button.

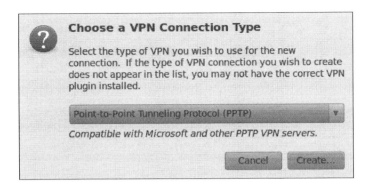

4. Add a **Connection name**. I'll call it **Matt's Network**.

5. Add a **Gateway**, this should resolve to the server IP you configured during PPTP setup. If the IP isn't directly accessible, you'll have to configure a NAT port forward rule.

6. Add the **User name** and **Password** you've configured:

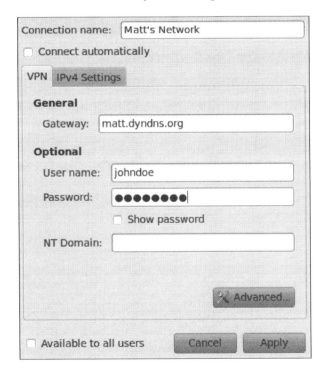

7. Click **Apply**.

8. Click **Close**.

9. Pull down the **Network connection** toolbar menu and choose **VPN Connections |
Matt's Network**:

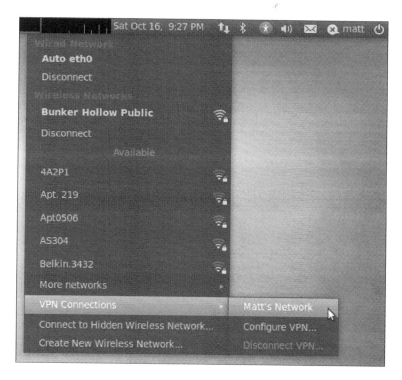

Connect from an Apple Mac OSx Client

Perform the following steps to create a PPTP VPN connection from a Mac OSx machine:

1. Open **System Preferences**:

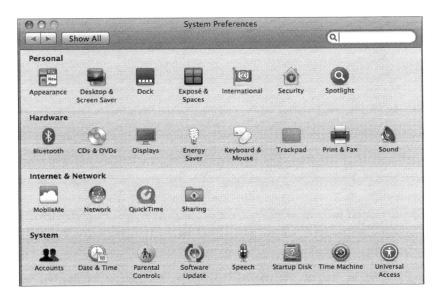

2. Click **Network**:

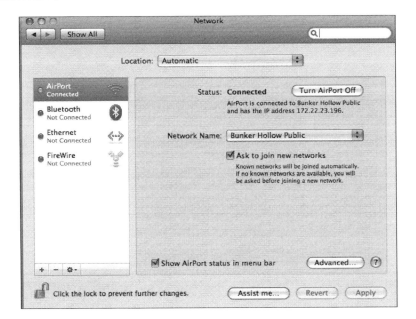

3. Click the "plus" button to add a new network connection.
4. Select the **VPN** as the **Interface**.
5. Select the **PPTP** as the **VPN Type**.
6. Create a **Service Name**, **Matt's Network**:

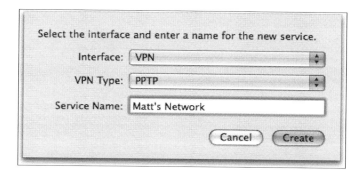

7. Specify **Server Address**, this should resolve to the Server IP you configured during PPTP setup. If the IP isn't directly accessible you'll have to configure a NAT port-forward rule.
8. Enter the username we'd configured in **Account Name**.
9. Click **Connect** and the password prompt will appear.

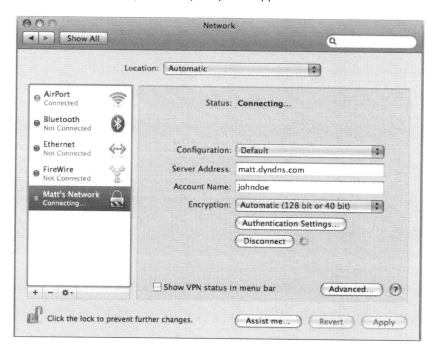

See also

- ▶ The *Creating a NAT port forward rule* recipe in *Chapter 3, General Configuration*
- ▶ The *Creating an IPsec VPN tunnel* recipe
- ▶ The *Configuring the L2TP VPN service* recipe
- ▶ The *Configuring the OpenVPN service* recipe

5
Advanced Configuration

In this chapter, we will cover:

- ▶ Creating a virtual IP
- ▶ Creating a 1:1 NAT rule
- ▶ Creating an outbound NAT rule
- ▶ Creating a gateway
- ▶ Creating a static route
- ▶ Configuring traffic-shaping (QoS, Quality of Service)
- ▶ Bridging interfaces
- ▶ Creating a virtual LAN
- ▶ Creating a captive portal

Introduction

The following recipes cover advanced networking features that are usually found only in enterprise-class software. However, every single one of these features is available in the latest version of pfSense.

Creating a virtual IP

This recipe describes how to create a virtual IP address in pfSense.

Getting ready

pfSense allows for four different types of virtual IP addresses to be created:

- **Proxy ARP**
- **CARP**
- **Other**
- **IP Alias**

A common use of virtual IPs is to configure a 1:1 NAT relationship. In this scenario a virtual IP of type **Other** is required, which we will configure in this recipe.

How to do it...

1. Browse to **Firewall | Virtual IPs**.
2. Click the "plus" button to add a new virtual IP address.
3. Choose **Other** as **Type**.
4. Select the **WAN** as the **Interface**.
5. Specify the **IP Address**.
6. Add a **Description**.

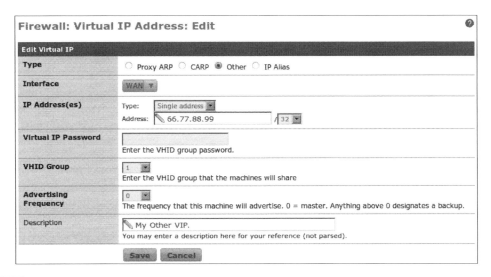

7. **Save** the changes.

8. **Apply** changes, if necessary.

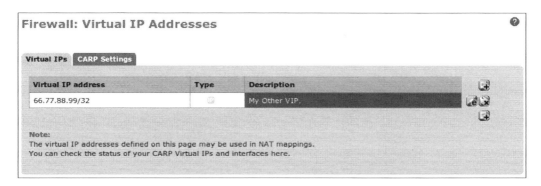

How it works...

A virtual IP (VIP) of type **Other** has the following properties:

▸ Traffic can only be forwarded to this type of VIP; pfSense cannot use this type of VIP for its own services

▸ The VIP may be in a different subnet than its interface

▸ The VIP cannot respond to pings

There's more...

We've configured a virtual IP of type **Other**, but there are three more types of virtual IP addresses that can be configured in pfSense 2.0. The four different types of virtual IP addresses are similar, but have slightly varied properties:

▸ **CARP**
  ❏ Can be used or forwarded by the firewall
  ❏ Uses Layer 2 traffic
  ❏ Should be used in firewall fail-over or load-balancing scenarios
  ❏ Must be in the same subnet as the interface
  ❏ Will respond to pings if configured properly

▸ **Proxy ARP**
  ❏ Can only be forwarded by the firewall
  ❏ Uses Layer 2 traffic
  ❏ Can be in a different subnet than the interface
  ❏ Cannot respond to pings

▶ **Other**
- ❏ Can only be forwarded by the firewall
- ❏ Can be in a different subnet than the interface
- ❏ Cannot respond to pings

▶ **IP Alias**
- ❏ New to pfSense 2.0
- ❏ Can be used or forwarded by the firewall
- ❏ Allows extra IP addresses to be added to an interface

Configuring a CARP virtual IP address

1. Browse to **Firewall | Virtual IPs**.
2. Click the "plus" button to add a new virtual IP address.
3. Choose **CARP** as **Type**.
4. Select **WAN** as the **Interface**.
5. Specify an **IP Address**.
6. Specify a **Virtual IP Password**.
7. Choose a **VHID Group**.
8. Choose an **Advertising Frequency** (**0** for **master**).
9. Add a **Description**:

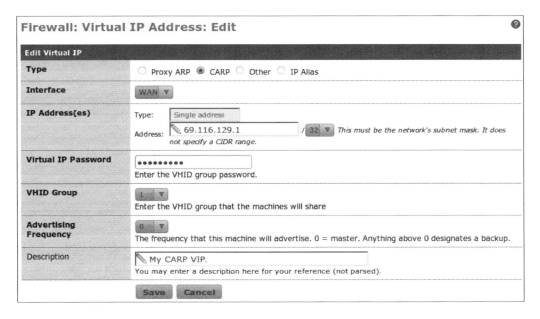

10. **Save** the changes.

11. **Apply** changes, if necessary.

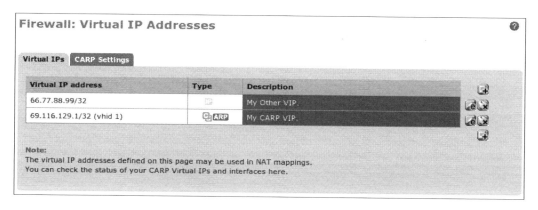

Configuring a Proxy ARP virtual IP address

1. Browse to **Firewall | Virtual IPs**.

2. Click the "plus" button to add a new virtual IP address.

3. Choose **Proxy ARP** as **Type**.

4. Select **WAN** as the **Interface**.

5. Select **Single address** as the **Type** of **IP Address**.

6. Specify an **IP Address**.

7. Add a **Description**:

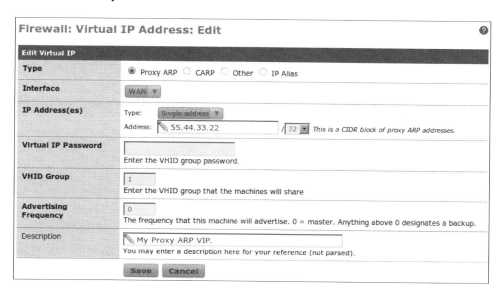

8. **Save** the changes.

9. **Apply** changes, if necessary.

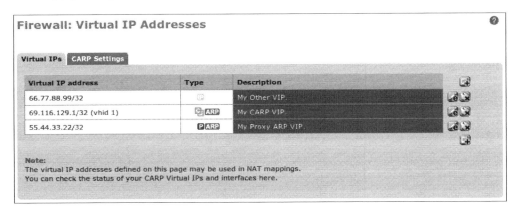

Configuring an IP alias virtual IP address

1. Browse to **Firewall | Virtual IPs**.

2. Click the "plus" button to add a new virtual IP address.

3. Choose **IP Alias Type**.

4. Select the **WAN Interface**.

5. Specify an **IP Address**.

6. Add a **Description**:

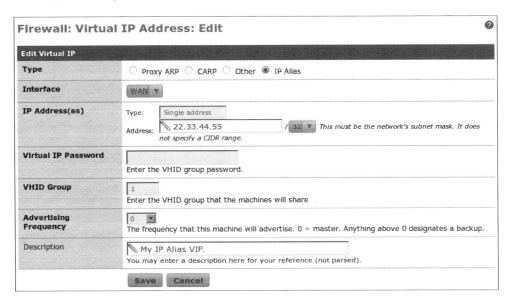

7. **Save** the changes.

8. **Apply** changes, if necessary.

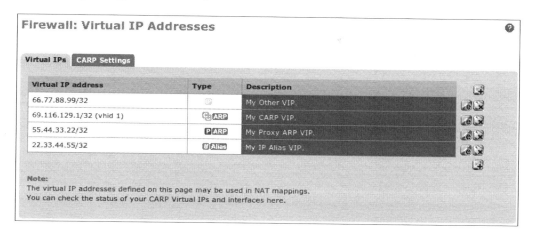

See also

▸ The *Configuring a 1:1 NAT rule* recipe

▸ The *Creating an outbound NAT rule* recipe

▸ The *Creating a static route* recipe

▸ The *Creating a virtual LAN* recipe

Configuring a 1:1 NAT rule

This recipe describes how to configure a 1:1 NAT rule. A **1:1 NAT rule** is used when you want to associate a public IP address with a single internal machine. Everything destined for the public IP will be routed to a single internal machine.

How to do it...

1. Browse to **Firewall | Virtual IPs**.

2. On the **Virtual IPs** tab, click the "plus" button to add a new virtual IP Address.

3. Select the **Proxy ARP** as the **Type**.

4. Select **WAN** as the **Interface**.

5. Select **Single address** as the **Type** of **IP Address** and specify our external public IP address.

6. Add a **Description**, such as **My public IP address**:

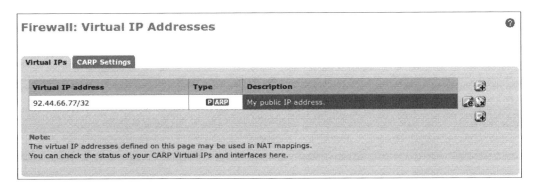

7. **Save** the changes.
8. **Apply** changes, if necessary.
9. Browse to **Firewall | NAT**.
10. Select the **1:1** tab.
11. Click the "plus" button to add a new 1:1 NAT rule.
12. Select an **Interface**, in this case **WAN**.
13. Specify a **Source**, in this case **any**.
14. Specify a **Destination**, we'll specify our internal webserver by alias.
15. Specify the **External subnet**, our public IP address.
16. Add a **Description**, such as **Forward all external requests to Webserver1**.
17. Leave **NAT reflection** disabled:

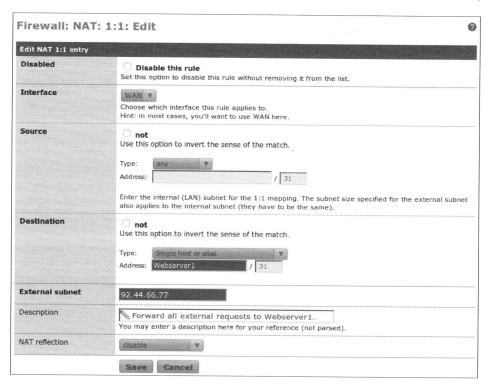

18. **Save** the changes.
19. **Apply** changes, if necessary.

How it works...

Once a 1:1 NAT relationship is established, all traffic will be forwarded to the internal IP address (or subnet), just as if the internal machine was directly configured with the public IP address. This is much easier than creating port-forward rules if all of your incoming traffic is destined for the same machine.

There's more...

Like many advanced networking features, 1:1 NAT relationships require the use of Virtual IP Addresses (VIPs).

See also

▶ The *Creating a virtual IP* recipe

Creating an outbound NAT rule

This recipe describes how to create an outbound NAT rule.

Getting ready

An outbound NAT rule defines how traffic *leaving* a network will be translated. This can be a difficult concept to grasp at first since most general networking scenarios are only concerned with where network packets are headed, not what they look like when they leave.

This recipe will describe how to use an outbound NAT rule to solve a common scenario which involves NATing to a single machine with multiple interfaces. We will assume that we have a single destination server with two interfaces—LAN and DMZ, and our pfSense firewall is protecting both interfaces. Using a regular old port-forward rule, we forward HTTP requests to the server on its DMZ interface, which is fine. However, when we try to forward SSH requests to the LAN interface of the server, traffic arrives correctly but tries to reply via the DMZ network. This fails to be recognized as valid by the firewall and we're left with a timeout when trying to connect.

The solution is to handle the SSH requests using an outbound NAT rule coupled with a 1:1 NAT rule, as described in the recipe.

How to do it...

1. Browse to **Firewall | Virtual IPs**.
2. On the **Virtual IPs** tab, click the "plus" button to add a new virtual IP address.
3. Select the **Proxy ARP** as the **Type**.
4. Select **WAN** as the **Interface**.
5. Select **Single address** as the **Type** of **IP Address** and specify our external public IP address.
6. Add a **Description**, such as **My public IP address**.
7. **Save** the changes.
8. **Apply** changes, if necessary.

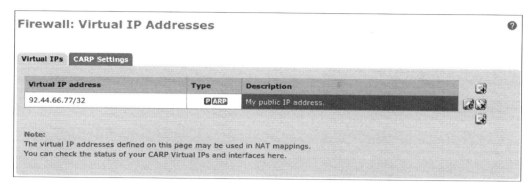

9. Browse to **Firewall | NAT**.

10. Click the **Outbound** tab.

11. Select **Automatic outbound NAT rule generation (IPsec passthrough included)** mode.

12. Click the "plus" button to add a new outbound NAT mapping.

13. Choose the **Interface** of the machine(s) that will respond, in this case **LAN**.

14. Specify **any** for **Source**.

15. Specify a **Destination**, the IP address of the server that will respond.

16. Leave **Translation** set to **Interface address** and specify port **22** to respond to SSH requests.

17. Enter a **Description**, such as **Outbound NAT for WAN Clients to Server1 SSH**.

18. **Save** the changes.

19. **Apply** changes, if necessary.

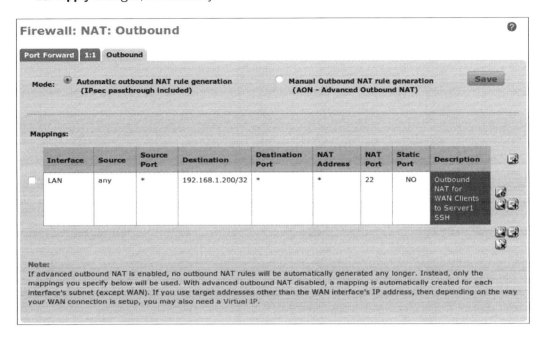

20. Browse to **Firewall | NAT**.

21. Click the **1:1** tab.

22. Click the "plus" button to add a new 1:1 NAT mapping.

23. Choose **WAN** as the **Interface**.

24. Select **any** for **Source**.

25. Specify a **Single host or Alias** for **Destination**, and provide the IP address of the server which will handle requests.

26. Specify the Virtual IP address we created earlier as the **External subnet**.

27. Add a **Description**, such as **1:1 NAT Public IP to Server1**.

28. **Save** the changes.

29. **Apply** changes, if necessary.

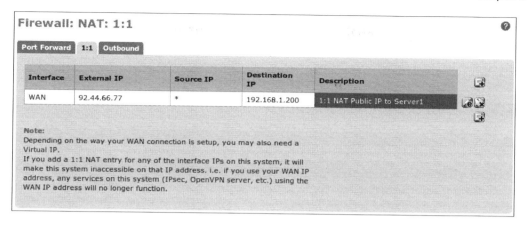

30. Browse to **Firewall | Rules**.
31. Click the **WAN** tab.
32. Click the "plus" button to add a new firewall rule.
33. Choose **any** for **Source**.
34. Choose **any** for **Source port range**.
35. Select **Single host or Alias** for **Destination** and specify the IP address or alias of the server that will handle requests.
36. Specify **SSH** for our **Destination port range**.
37. Add a **Description**, such as **Allow WAN Clients to Server1 SSH**.
38. **Save** the changes.

39. **Apply** changes, if necessary.

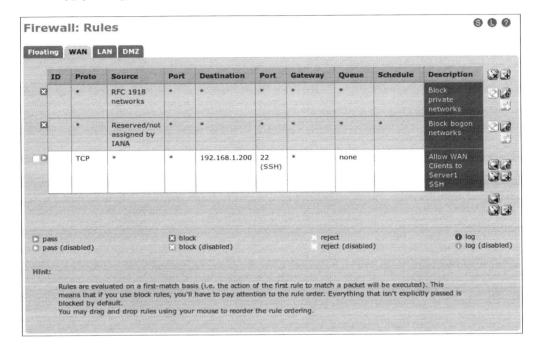

How it works...

The outbound rule we've created explicitly tells pfSense to direct outgoing traffic through the LAN interface, regardless of which interface it came in on. This will allow SSH traffic to find its way home even though the default gateway of the server is configured for another interface (the DMZ). Meanwhile, the HTTP requests that have been configured through port-forwarding will continue to function normally.

See also

- ▶ The *Creating a virtual IP* recipe
- ▶ The *Creating a 1:1 NAT rule* recipe
- ▶ The *Configuring a port-forward rule* recipe

Creating a gateway

This recipe describes how to create a gateway in pfSense.

Getting ready

Typically, networks with a single WAN connection will not need to modify gateway settings; the default will suffice. However, networks that have more than one internet connection or take advantage of certain advanced features (for example static routes) will need to define custom gateways.

How to do it...

1. Go to **System | Routing**.
2. Click the **Gateways** tab.
3. Click the "plus" button to add a new gateway.
4. Select the **Interface** for the new gateway.
5. Specify a **Name** for the gateway (no spaces allowed).
6. Specify the IP address for the gateway—it must be a valid address on the chosen interface.
7. We may assign an alternative **Monitor IP**, or leave it blank to be filled with the gateway's IP address by default.
8. Add a **Description**, such as **My new gateway**:

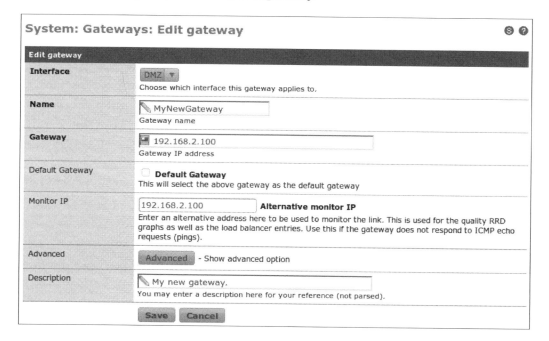

9. **Save** the changes.

10. **Apply** changes, if necessary.

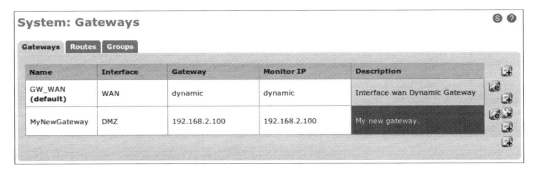

How it works...

A gateway is the "portal" which connects two networks together. Traffic between two networks, such as between our LAN and the Internet, must pass through a gateway. If we had multiple WAN connections (that is multiple connections to the Internet) we would need to define gateways for each.

There's more...

As we'll see in the next recipe, gateways are necessary when creating static routes. A static route is a hard-coded pathway from one network to another, and all inter-network traffic must pass through a gateway.

Gateway Groups

PfSense 2.0 implements a new concept called Gateway Groups. A **Gateway Group** is a collection of gateways that can be treated as one unit from various other features in the system.

Gateway groups will appear in the gateway drop-down menu when appropriate, such as when defining a firewall rule.

See also

▶ The *Creating a firewall rule* recipe in *Chapter 3, General Configuration*

▶ The *Configuring the WAN interface* recipe in *Chapter 1, Initial Configuration*

▶ The *Creating a static route* recipe

Creating a static route

This recipe describes how to create a static route using pfSense.

Getting ready

Static routes are for accessing networks that aren't reachable through the default WAN gateway, but can be reached indirectly through a difference interface. A common scenario might be an office building with a shared network for printing. Anyone connected to the business network can use the shared network, they just need to create a static route. We can use pfSense to create this static route for an entire interface, instead of a configuring a static route on each individual PC.

How to do it...

1. Browse to **System | Routing**.
2. Click the **Gateways** tab.
3. Click the "plus" button to add a new gateway.
4. Select the **Interface** for the new gateway.
5. Specify a **Name** for the gateway (no spaces allowed).
6. Specify the **IP address** for the gateway; it must be a valid address on the chosen interface.
7. We may assign an alternative **Monitor IP**, or leave blank to be filled with the gateway's IP address by default.
8. Add a **Description**, such as **My new gateway**.
9. **Save** the changes.
10. **Apply** changes, if necessary.

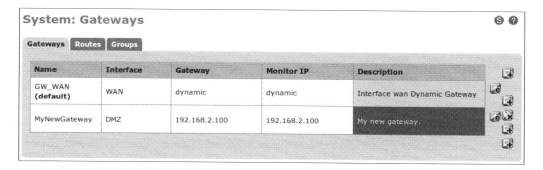

11. Browse to **System | Routing**.

12. Click the **Routes** tab.

13. Click the "plus" button to add a new route.

14. Enter the IP Address of the **Destination** network.

15. Choose the **Gateway** we've defined above.

16. Add a **Description**, such as **Static route for shared printer network**.

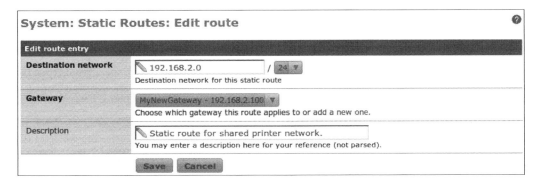

17. **Save** the changes.

18. **Apply** changes, if necessary.

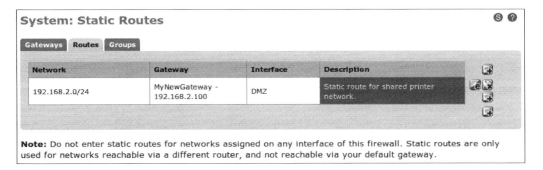

How it works...

By defining a static route, we have hard-coded a path to our shared printer network. We can now access this network through this static route, and offer this gateway to other users of the firewall.

▸ The *Creating a gateway* recipe

Configuring traffic-shaping (QoS, Quality of Service)

This recipe describes how to configure traffic-shaping in pfSense.

Getting ready

Traffic-shaping, also known as **Quality of Service** (**QoS**), is the prioritization and throttling of network packets. Prioritizing network packets gives certain types of traffic precedence over others. Throttling network packets sets limits to the amount of certain types of traffic for any given time. An administrator may want to prioritize VoIP packets over all others to ensure phone calls aren't dropped or interrupted due to high network traffic. Additionally, we may also want to limit VoIP throughput to 100Kbps. This is a fairly typical example of shaping VoIP traffic

In the following recipe, we will use pfSense to shape the external Remote Desktop (MSRDP) connections coming into our network. This will ensure that we will be able to remotely administer our servers even under heavy loads.

How to do it...

1. Browse to **Firewall | Traffic Shaper**.
2. Click the **Wizards** tab.
3. Of the **Wizard functions**, click **Single WAN multi LAN**.

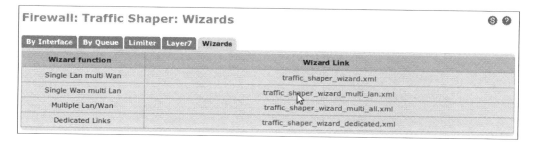

115

4. Enter our number of LAN type connections in **Enter number of LAN type connections**. Our pfSense box has a LAN and a DMZ; so we'll enter **2**.

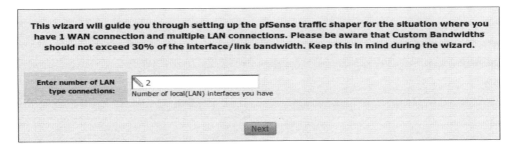

5. Enter the **Link Upload** speed of our WAN connection. Our ISP provides us a 2,000Kbps (2Mbps) upload speed. Check `http://speedtest.net/` for an accurate measurement.

6. Enter the **Link Download** speed of our WAN connection. Our ISP provides us a 15,000Kbps (15Mbps) download speed. Check `http://speedtest.net/` for an accurate measurement.

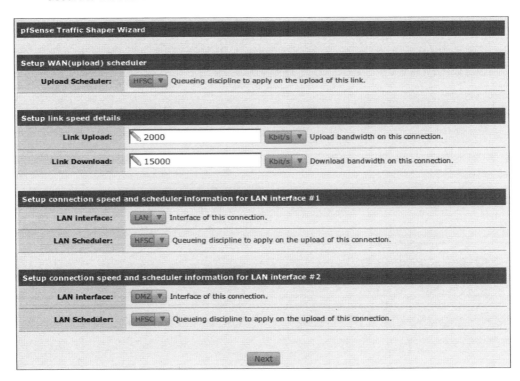

7. The next page is specifically for shaping **VoIP traffic**, which we'll skip by clicking **Next**.

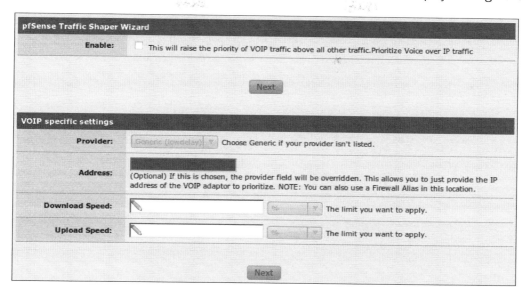

8. The next page, **PenaltyBox**, allows us to reduce the priority of a particular IP address or alias. This can be very useful, but we have no need for it at the moment and can skip it by clicking **Next**.

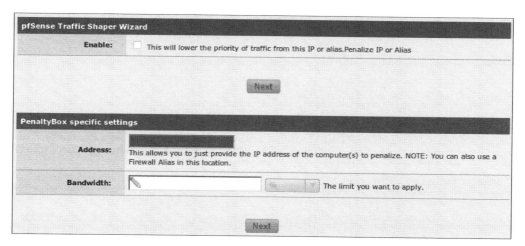

9. **Peer to Peer** (**P2P**) **Networking** can lower the priority and throttle all P2P traffic, or roughly 20 pre-defined popular P2P networks. We'll continue on by clicking **Next**:

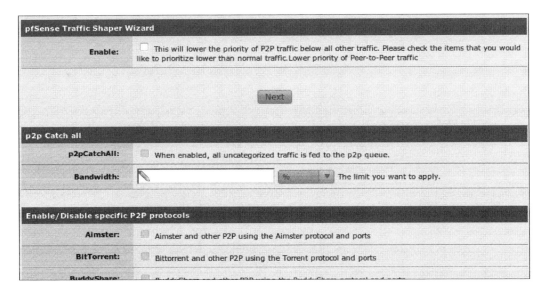

10. **Network Games** allows us to shape network gaming traffic. Roughly 20 popular gaming types are pre-defined. Click **Next** to continue:

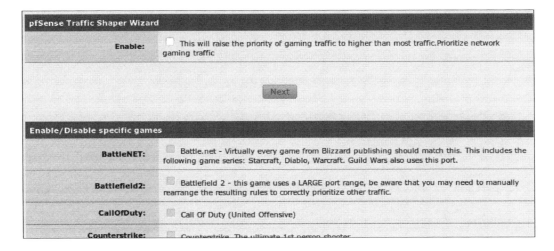

11. The final page, **Other Applications**, allows us to shape other common types of traffic. Here we will click the checkbox to **Enable** other-application shaping and then set **MSRDP** to a **Higher priority**. Click **Next** to continue:

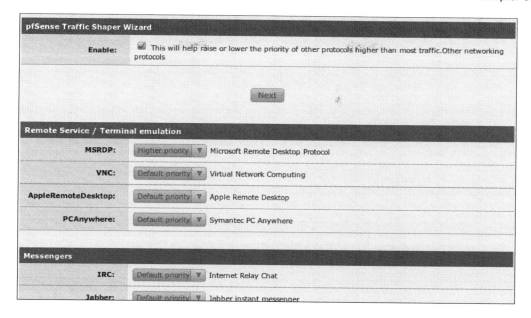

12. Click **Finish** to apply the new settings:

After pressing Finish the system will load the new profile.
Please note that this may take a moment.
Also note that the traffic shaper is stateful meaning that only new connections will be shaped.
If this is an issue please reset the state table after loading the profile.

pfSense Traffic Shaper Wizard

Finish

How it works...

Using the traffic-shaping wizard, we have defined a set of rules that will prioritize remote desktop traffic above all others. Even if the network is under heavy web, VoIP, or any other type of traffic, our remote desktop connections will perform well and be uninterrupted since they have been given priority.

Bridging interfaces

This recipe describes how to bridge together two interfaces in pfSense. Bridging allows you to join two networks together. For example, a network administrator may want to bridge a wired network with a wireless network.

How to do it...

1. Browse to **Interfaces | (assign)**.
2. Click the **Bridges** tab.
3. Click the "plus" button to create a new bridge.
4. Select the **Member Interfaces** with *Ctrl* + click.
5. Add a **Description**, such as **LAN DMZ Bridge**:

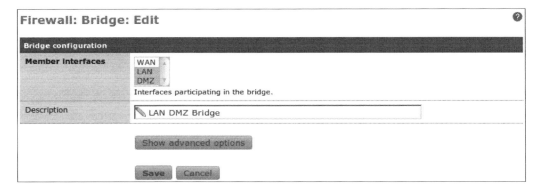

6. **Save** the changes:

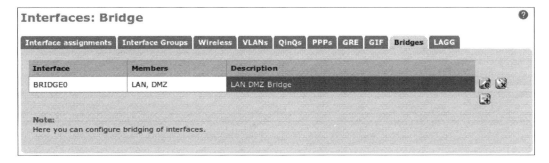

How it works...

Bridging combines two interfaces on the firewall into a single Layer-2 network. Our LAN and DMZ interfaces are now connected.

There's more...

Click the **Show advanced options** button to configure any of the following:

- RSTP/STP: Enable spanning tree options
  - Protocol
  - STP Interfaces
  - Valid time
  - Forward time
  - Hello time
  - Priority
  - Hold count
  - Interface priority
  - Path cost
- Cache size
- Cache entry expire time
- Span port
- Edge ports
- Auto Edge ports
- PTP ports
- Auto PTP ports
- Sticky ports
- Private ports

See also

- The _Identifying and assigning interfaces_ recipe in _Chapter 1, Initial Configuration_

Creating a virtual LAN

This recipe describes how to create a virtual LAN in pfSense.

Getting ready

A VLAN allows a single physical switch to host multiple Layer-2 networks by separating ports with VLAN tags. A VLAN tag defines a separate virtual network. The pfSense firewall can attach to each VLAN by defining VLAN tags on the firewall interfaces.

How to do it...

1. Browse to **Interfaces | (assign)**.
2. Click the **VLANs** tab.
3. Click the "plus" button to add a new virtual LAN.
4. Select a **Parent Interface**. Refer to the interface assignment page as a reference (shown in the following screenshot). In this case, **DMZ** is assigned to interface **vr2** and we'll select that.

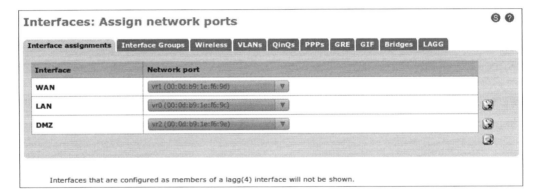

5. Specify a **VLAN tag**, any integer from 1 to 4094.
6. Add a **Description**, such as **My DMZ virtual LAN**.

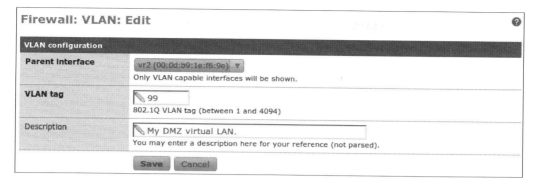

7. **Save** the changes.

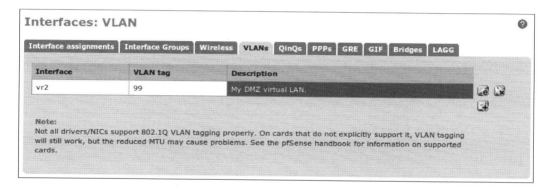

How it works...

Every packet destined for, or originating from our VLAN will be marked with the VLAN tag. This is how pfSense differentiates them from other network traffic and ensures they end up in the right place.

See also

▶ The *Identifying and assigning interfaces* recipe in *Chapter 1, Initial Configuration*

Creating a captive portal

This recipe describes how to create a captive portal with pfSense.

Getting ready

A **captive portal** is a web page that is displayed before a user is allowed to browse the web. This is most often seen at commercial Wi-Fi hotspots where you must pay for service before you are allowed to surf the web. In other scenarios, captive portals are used for authentication or end-user agreements.

During this recipe, we will configure pfSense to display an authentication captive portal before users are allowed to surf the web from our DMZ.

How to do it...

1. Browse to **Services | Captive Portal**.
2. From the **Captive portal** tab, click **Enable captive portal**.
3. Choose **Interfaces**; we'll select our DMZ as our interface.
4. Specify an **Idle timeout**; we'll say **10** minutes.
5. Specify a **Hard timeout**; we'll leave the default of **60** minutes.
6. Click **Enable logout popup window** so that users may log themselves out when they are finished.
7. Specify a **Redirection URL**, say **http://www.google.com**.

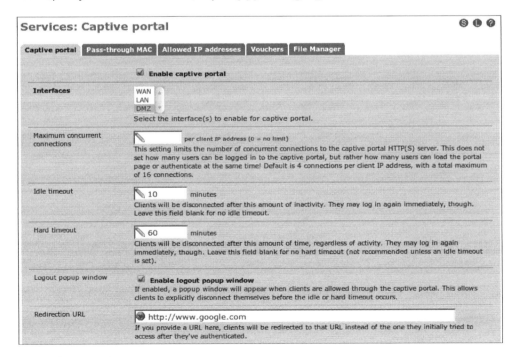

8. Select **Local User Manager** as the **Authentication**:

9. **Save** the changes.
10. Browse to **System | User Manager**.
11. Click the **Users** tab.
12. Click the "plus" button to add a new user.
13. Enter a **Username**.
14. Enter and confirm a **Password**.
15. Enter a **Full name**:

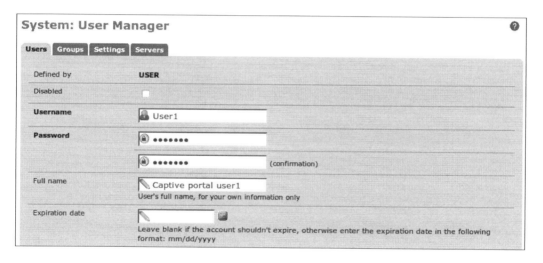

16. **Save** the changes:

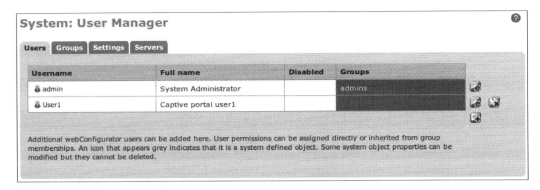

How it works...

By creating a captive portal on the DMZ as described, any user who attempts to browse the web will first have to authenticate on the following page. Once authenticated, they will be directed to Google, where they may surf the web before they encounter a timeout we have defined, at which point they will have to authenticate on the following page once again.

pfSense captive portal

Welcome to the pfSense Captive Portal! This is the default page since a custom page has not been defined.

Username: _____
Password: _____

[Continue]

There's more...

All three captive portal pages (login, logout and error) can be customized to fit your organization's styling. The easiest way to do this is to save each page as a file, edit it to your liking (without changing form, input IDs, or names), and then upload it using the options at the bottom of the **Captive Portal service** page.

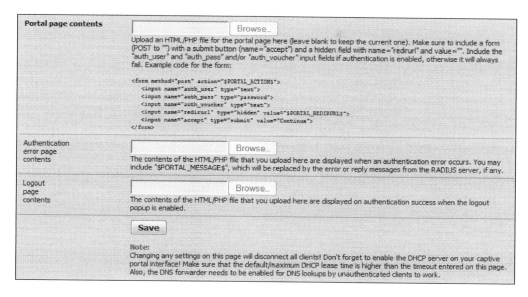

6
Redundancy, Load Balancing, and Failover

In this chapter, we will cover:

- ▸ Configuring multiple WAN interfaces
- ▸ Configuring multi-WAN load balancing
- ▸ Configuring multi-WAN failover
- ▸ Configuring a web server load balancer
- ▸ Configuring a web server failover
- ▸ Configuring CARP firewall failover

Introduction

Redundancy, load-balancing, and failover are some of the most advanced features of modern networking. They are generally only necessary or required within large or sensitive systems and not all firewall and router products support these types of configurations. pfSense, of course, supports them all.

Redundant WAN interfaces (multi-WAN) provide a single firewall with multiple independent connections to the Internet. pfSense can then be configured to load-balance or failover the multi-WAN interfaces. Load-balancing would divide all traffic among the interfaces while failover would use a single interface, but upon failover it would automatically switch to another.

The pfSense load balancer allows for specific types of traffic (for example, web traffic) to be distributed among multiple servers. The ability to create your own webfarm is built right into pfSense!

Redundant firewalls allow the system to survive the death of a physical firewall machine. Using a CARP configuration, pfSense can be configured to failover to a backup firewall in case the primary dies.

Configuring multiple WAN interfaces

This recipe describes how to configure multiple WAN interfaces in pfSense.

Getting ready

A pfSense system with a single WAN interface is nearly plug-and-play since a default gateway is created automatically. However, some of the recipes in this chapter require multiple WAN connections and those gateways must be configured manually. The following recipe describes how to configure two WAN interfaces which can be used later for redundant load balancing and/or failover.

 The following interfaces will be configured with private IP addresses for the purpose of this example, but an actual configuration would require each WAN interface to be properly configured using the settings provided by their respective ISPs.

How to do it...

1. Browse to **System | Routing**.
2. Select the **Gateways** tab.
3. Take note that the gateway for our existing WAN interface was created automatically, set as **default**, and usually set as **dynamic**:

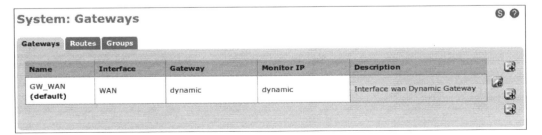

4. Click the "plus" button to add a new gateway.

5. Choose the **Interface** for our existing WAN connection.

6. Specify a **Name** for the gateway.

7. Specify the **Gateway** IP address.

8. Check **Default Gateway**.

9. Add a **Description**, such as **WAN Gateway**:

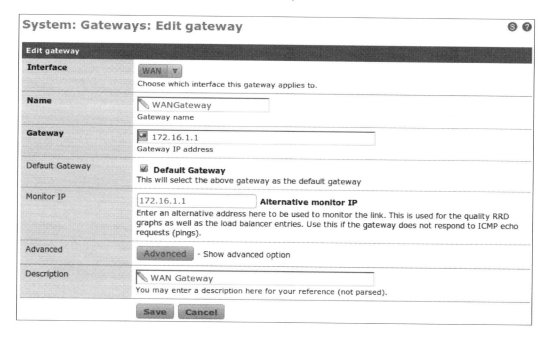

10. **Save** the changes:

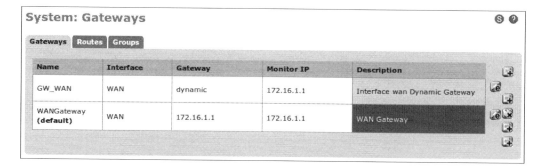

11. Click the "plus" button to add a new gateway.

12. Choose the **Interface** for our new WAN connection.

13. Specify a **Name** for the gateway.

14. Specify the **Gateway** IP address.

15. Add a **Description**, such as **WAN2 gateway:**

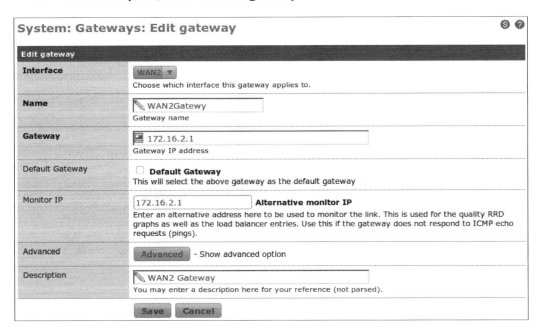

16. **Save** the changes.

17. **Apply** changes, if necessary.

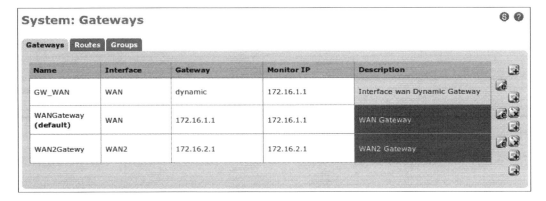

18. Browse to **Interfaces | WAN**.

19. Choose **Static** as the **Type**:

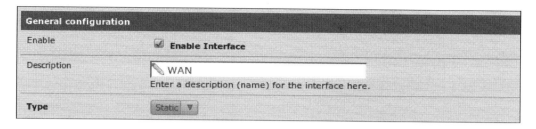

20. Specify an **IP Address**.

21. Select our newly created **Gateway**.

22. Check **Block private networks**.

23. Check **Block bogon networks**:

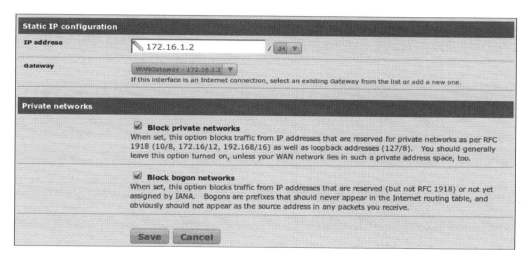

24. **Save** the changes.

25. Browse to **Interfaces | WAN2**.

26. Choose **Static** as the **Type**:

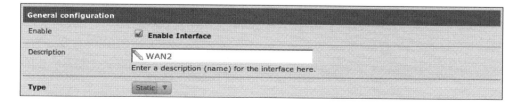

27. Specify an **IP Address**.

28. Select our newly created **Gateway**.

29. Check **Block private networks**.

30. Check **Block bogon networks**:

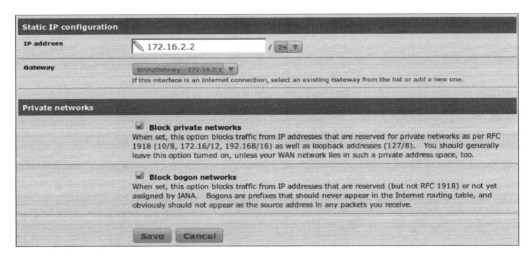

31. **Save** the changes.

32. **Apply** changes, if necessary.

How it works...

Only the first WAN interface created in pfSense will create an automatically generated default gateway. By creating a manual gateway for our new WAN interface, as we've just done, we can now properly configure that interface for the available redundancy features described throughout the rest of this chapter.

There's more...

Remember to block private and bogon networks for WAN interfaces in public network ranges.

See also

- ▶ The *Configuring interfaces* recipe in *Chapter 1, Initial Configuration*
- ▶ The *Creating a gateway* recipe in *Chapter 5, Advanced Configuration*
- ▶ The *Configuring multi-WAN load balancing* recipe
- ▶ The *Configuring multi-WAN failover* recipe

Configuring multi-WAN load balancing

This recipe describes how to configure multi-WAN load balancing on a single pfSense system.

Getting ready

Throughout this recipe, we will configure load-balancing for two separate WAN interfaces. Make sure that the WAN interfaces are first properly configured; refer to the previous recipe for the specifics.

 Every time multi-WAN load balancing is in effect, failover is as well. If we wanted to enable multi-WAN failover only, we would refer to the next recipe.

How to do it...

1. Browse to **System | Routing**.
2. Select the **Groups** tab.
3. Enter a **Group Name**.
4. Set the **Gateway Priority** of both our WAN gateways to **Tier 1**.
5. Leave the **Trigger Level** set to **Member Down**.
6. Add a **Description**:

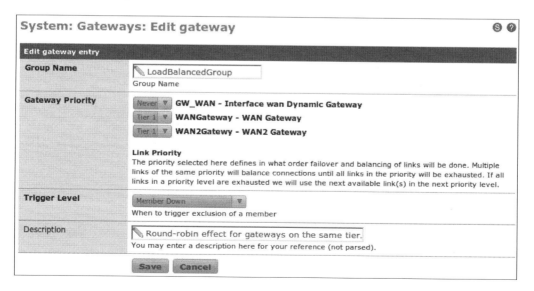

7. **Save** the changes.

8. **Apply** changes, if necessary:

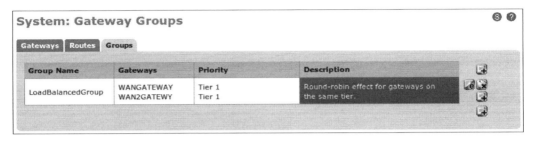

9. Browse to **System | Routing**.

10. Edit our WAN gateway.

11. Specify an external IP address that responds to pings in the **Monitor IP** field. I have chosen the IP for `http://www.google.com/` in this example, but you may prefer to choose an address closer to your firewall for the sake of performance (an IP within your ISP network perhaps).

12. **Save** the changes.

13. Edit our WAN2 gateway.

14. Specify an external IP address that responds to pings in the **Monitor IP** field. I have chosen the IP for `http://www.yahoo.com/` in this example.

15. **Save** the changes.

16. **Apply** changes, if necessary:

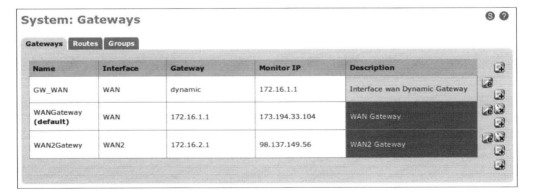

17. Browse to **Firewall | Rules**.

18. Click the "plus" button to create a new firewall rule.

19. Select the **pass** action.

20. Ensure the LAN interface is selected.

21. Set the **Protocol** to **any**.

22. Set the **Source** to **LAN subnet**.

23. Set the **Destination** to **any**.

24. Add a **Description**.

25. In **Advanced Features**, under **Gateway**, click the **Advanced** button to show advanced gateway features.

26. Set **Gateway** to **LoadBalancedGroup**.

27. **Save** the changes.

28. **Apply** changes, if necessary.

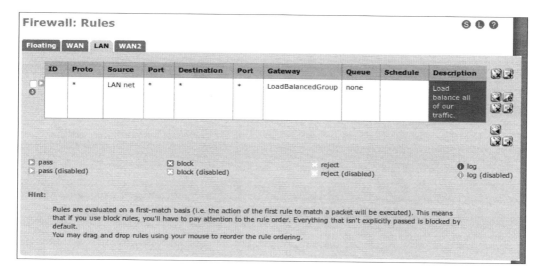

How it works...

All traffic from our LAN will pass through our gateway group. Since our gateway group consists of our two WAN gateways on the same level of priority, they will alternate back and forth in a round-robin type style.

Also, by monitoring external IP addresses on each gateway, pfSense will know when a gateway is down and exclude that member from the group. Every time load-balancing is used, failover is also in effect by default.

There's more...

We've defined our gateway group to trigger on **Member Down**, but there are several other options:

► **Member Down**: Triggered when the **Monitor IP** defined in the gateway's settings stops responding to ICMP pings

► **Packet Loss**: Triggered when packets traveling through this gateway are lost

► **High Latency**: Triggered when packets traveling through this gateway experience high latency

► **Packet Loss** or **High Latency**: Triggered when packets traveling through this gateway are lost or experience high latency

See also

► The *Configuring multiple WAN interfaces* recipe

Configuring multi-WAN failover

This recipe describes how to configure multi-WAN failover on a single pfSense system.

Getting ready

Throughout this recipe, we will configure failover for our two separate WAN interfaces. Make sure that the WAN interfaces are first properly configured; refer to the previous recipe for the specifics.

How to do it...

1. Browse to **System | Routing**.
2. Select the **Groups** tab.
3. Enter a **Group Name**.
4. Set the **Gateway Priority** of our WAN gateway to **Tier 1**.
5. Set the **Gateway Priority** of our WAN2 gateway to **Tier 2**.
6. Leave the **Trigger Level** set to **Member Down**.
7. Add a **Description**:

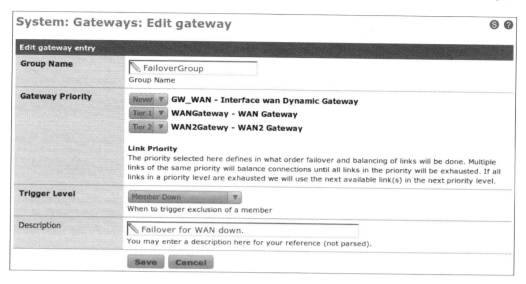

8. **Save** the changes.

9. **Apply** changes, if necessary:

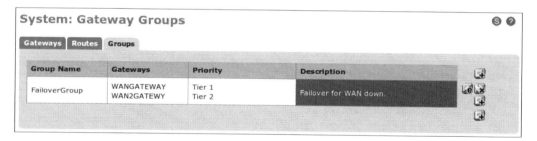

10. Browse to **System | Routing**.

11. **Edit** our WAN gateway.

12. Specify an external IP address that responds to pings in the **Monitor IP** field. I chose the IP for google.com in this example.

13. **Save** the changes.

14. **Edit** our WAN2 gateway.

15. Specify an external IP address that responds to pings in the **Monitor IP** field. I chose the IP for yahoo.com in this example.

16. **Save** the changes.

17. **Apply** changes, if necessary:

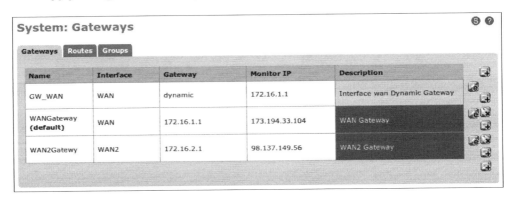

18. Browse to **Firewall | Rules**.

19. Click the "plus" button to create a new firewall rule.

20. Select the **Pass Action**.

21. Ensure the LAN interface is selected.

22. Set the **Protocol** to **any**.

23. Set the **Source** to **LAN subnet**.

24. Set the **Destination** to **any**.

25. Add a **Description**.

26. In **Advanced Features**, under **Gateway**, click the **Advanced** button to show advanced gateway features.

27. Set **Gateway** to **FailoverGroup**.

28. **Save** the changes.

29. **Apply** the changes:

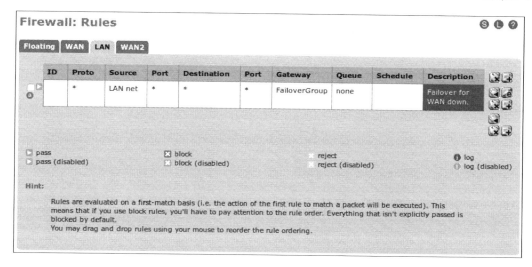

How it works...

All traffic from our LAN will pass through our gateway group. Since our gateway group consists of two WAN gateways on separate priority levels, our backup gateway (**Tier 2**) will kick into place when our primary gateway (**Tier 1**) goes down.

There's more...

We've defined our gateway group to trigger on **Member Down**, but there are several other options:

- ▶ **Member Down**: Triggered when the Monitor IP defined in the gateway's settings stops responding to ICMP pings

- ▶ **Packet Loss**: Triggered when packets traveling through this gateway are lost

- ▶ **High Latency**: Triggered when packets traveling through this gateway experience high latency

- ▶ **Packet Loss** or **High Latency**: Triggered when packets traveling through this gateway are lost or experience high latency

See also

- ▶ The *Configuring multiple WAN interfaces* recipe
- ▶ The *Configuring multi-WAN load balancing* recipe

Configuring a web server load balancer

This recipe describes how to configure a small webfarm using the pfSense load balancer.

Getting ready

The load balancer allows pfSense to distribute certain types of traffic to multiple machines. A common use of this feature is to distribute incoming HTTP requests to multiple webservers and the following recipe describes how the load balancer can create a webfarm to accomplish this.

How to do it...

1. Browse to **Services | Load Balancer**.
2. Click the **Monitor** tab.
3. Click the "plus" button to add a new monitor.
4. Specify a **Name**.
5. Add a **Description**.
6. Set **Type** to **HTTP**.
7. Set **Host** to an unused IP address that you will later use as the IP address for the virtual server. The virtual server will be configured to pass requests to the actual servers in the webfarm; so we will monitor this IP address.
8. Leave **HTTP Code** set to **200 OK**:

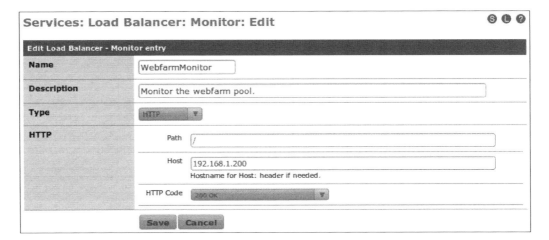

9. **Save** the changes.

10. **Apply** changes, if necessary:

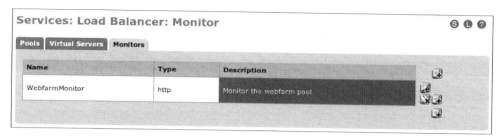

11. Click the **Pools** tab.

12. Click the "plus" button to add a new pool.

13. Specify a **Name**.

14. Set the **Mode** to **Load Balance**.

15. Add a **Description**.

16. Set the **Port** to **80** (since we're creating a webserver load balancer).

17. Set **Monitor** to our newly created **WebfarmMonitor**.

18. Specify the **Server IP Address** of each webserver in the farm and click **Add to pool**:

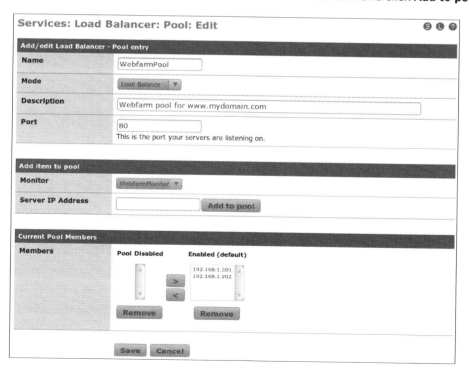

19. **Save** the changes.

20. **Apply** changes, if necessary:

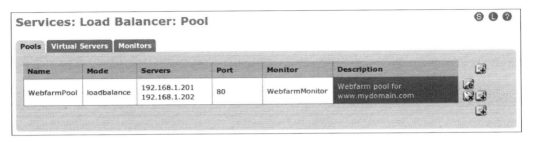

21. Click the **Virtual Servers** tab.

22. Click the "plus" button to add a new virtual server.

23. Specify a **Name**.

24. Add a **Description**.

25. Set the **IP Address** to the same IP address we chose for our newly created **WebfarmMonitor**.

26. Set **Port** to **80** (since we're dealing with a webserver load balancer).

27. Set **Virtual Server Pool** to our newly created **WebfarmPool**:

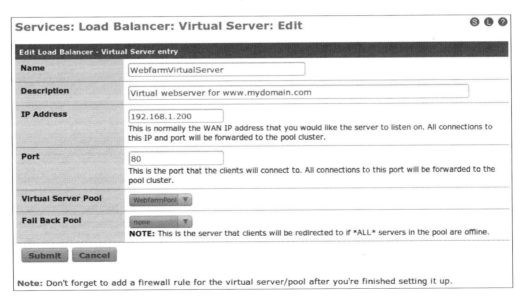

28. **Submit** the changes.

29. **Apply** changes, if necessary.

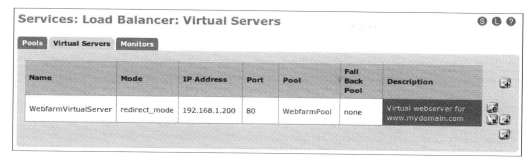

How it works...

Throughout this recipe, we've configured pfSense to divide incoming HTTP (port 80) traffic among two separate webservers. Our pool defines the location of the webservers and the load balance mode (as opposed to failover). Our virtual server defines the IP address we will use in our NAT and firewall rules to listen for the HTTP requests, which the virtual server will know to distribute equally to all the servers defined in our pool. The monitor will check the status of the pool by periodically making a web request. Since the request is directed to the virtual server's IP address, it will take the pool offline if any of the servers in the farm doesn't respond with a **200 OK** status. Since this is the case, we may want to define a failover pool as well.

There's more

Sticky connections can be used to ensure that the client will always make requests to the same server during a given length of time. If the next request is made after the "sticky connection timeout" length, then that request could be handled by any server in the farm.

Developers often need this feature to ensure the integrity of webserver specific data (in-memory cache), but it is not as reliable as using shared session storage.

See also

- ▶ The *Creating a NAT port forward rule* recipe in *Chapter 3, General Configuration*
- ▶ The *Creating a firewall rule* recipe in *Chapter 3, General Configuration*
- ▶ The *Configuring a web server failover* recipe

Configuring a web server failover

This recipe describes how to configure a small webfarm using the pfSense load balancer.

Getting ready

The load balancer also allows pfSense to send traffic to a failover server in case of downtime. In the following recipe, we will configure a backup webserver to take place of the primary in the event of downtime.

How to do it...

1. Browse to **Services | Load Balancer**.
2. Click the **Monitor tab**.
3. Click the "plus" button to add a new monitor.
4. Specify a **Name**.
5. Add a **Description**.
6. Set **Type** to **HTTP**.
7. Set **Host** to the IP address of our primary webserver.
8. Leave **HTTP Code** set to **200 OK**:

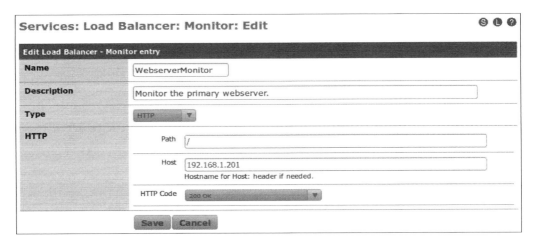

9. **Save** the changes.
10. **Apply** changes, if necessary:

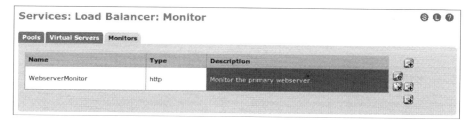

11. Click the **Pools** tab.

12. Click the "plus" button to add a new pool.

13. Specify a **Name**.

14. Set the **Mode** to **Manual Failover**.

15. Add a **Description**.

16. Set the **Port** to **80** (since we're creating a webserver failover).

17. Set **Monitor** to our newly created **WebFailoverMonitor**.

18. Specify the **Server IP Address** of the primary webserver and click **Add to pool**. The IP address will appear in the **Enabled (default)** list.

19. Specify the **Server IP Address** of the backup webserver and click **Add to pool**. The IP address will appear in the **Pool Disabled** list:

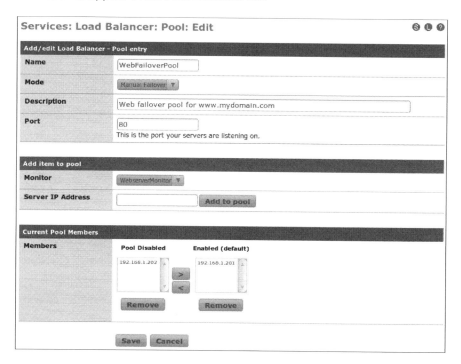

20. **Save** the changes.

21. **Apply** changes, if necessary:

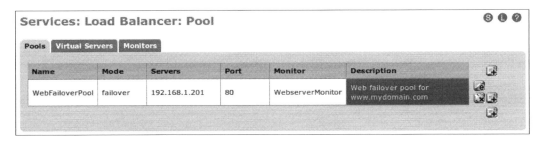

22. Click the **Virtual Servers** tab.

23. Click the "plus" button to add a new virtual server.

24. Specify a **Name**.

25. Add a **Description**.

26. Set the **IP Address** to an unused IP address.

27. Set **Port** to **80** (since we're dealing with a webserver failover).

28. Set **Virtual Server Pool** to our newly created **WebFailoverPool**:

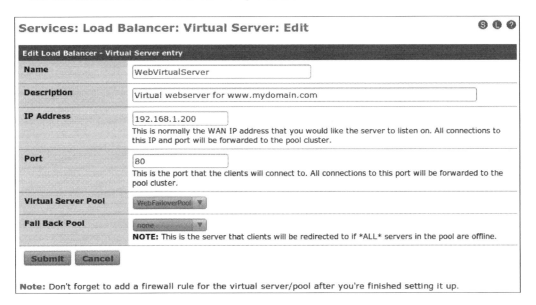

29. **Submit** the changes.

30. **Apply** changes, if necessary:

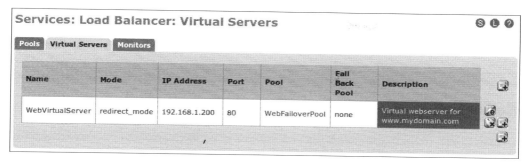

How it works...

Throughout this recipe, we've configured pfSense to automatically redirect traffic from the primary webserver to the backup webserver in the event of a failure. Our pool defines the location of the webservers and the failover mode (as opposed to load balance). Our virtual server defines the IP address we will use in our NAT and firewall rules to listen for the HTTP requests, which the virtual server redirects to the pool we've defined. The monitor will check on the status of the primary webserver by periodically making a web request. If the response coming back is **200 OK**, then the pool will send traffic to the primary server; otherwise, it will send traffic to the backup server.

See also

- ▸ The *Creating a NAT port forward rule* recipe in *Chapter 3, General Configuration*
- ▸ The *Creating a firewall rule* recipe in *Chapter 3, General Configuration*
- ▸ The *Configuring a web server load balancer* recipe

Configuring CARP firewall failover

This recipe describes how to configure two pfSense firewalls for failover.

Getting ready

Hardware redundancy requires additional hardware, of course. To configure a firewall failover, we will need two separate and identical pfSense machines. We also want each machine to have an additional interface dedicated to the syncing process (which we'll refer to as **pfsync**). The example in this recipe will utilize two separate pfSense firewall appliances, each with three interfaces (WAN, LAN, and pfsync).

The following interfaces will be configured with private IP addresses for the purposes of this example, but an actual configuration would require each WAN interface to be properly configured using the settings provided by their respective ISPs.

How to do it...

1. Configure the interfaces of our first machine, **primary-pfsense**, as follows:
   - ❏ **WAN**: 192.168.111.2
   - ❏ **SYNC**: 192.168.222.2
   - ❏ **LAN**: 192.168.1.2

2. Configure the interfaces of our second machine, **backup-pfsense**, as follows:
   - ❏ **WAN**: 192.168.111.3
   - ❏ **SYNC**: 192.168.222.3
   - ❏ **LAN**: 192.168.1.3

3. On both machines, add a firewall to allow all traffic on the SYNC interface:
   1. Browse to **Firewall | Rules**.
   2. Click the **SYNC Interface** tab.
   3. Click the "plus" button to add a new firewall rule.
   4. Set **Protocol** to **any**.

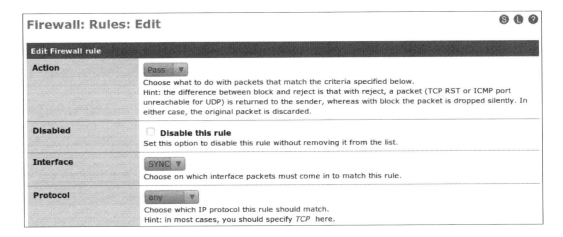

   4. Add a **Description**:

5. **Save** the changes.

6. **Apply** changes, if necessary.

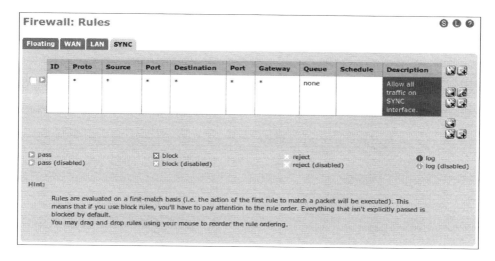

7. On the backup-pfsense machine, we need to enable CARP synchronization and configure it as a backup only:

1. Browse to **Firewall | Virtual IPs**.

2. Click the **CARP Settings** tab.

3. Check **Synchronize Enabled**.

4. Set **Synchronize Interface** to **SYNC**.

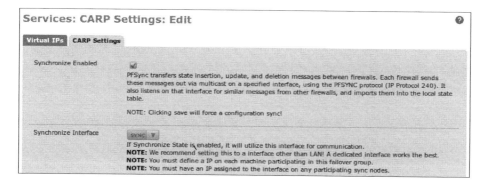

8. **Save** the changes.

9. We have now finished configuring the backup firewall.

10. On the primary-pfsense machine, we need to enable CARP synchronization and configure it to act as the primary firewall:

   1. Browse to **Firewall | Virtual IPs**.

   2. Click the **CARP Settings** tab.

   3. Check **Synchronize Enabled**.

   4. Set **Synchronize Interface** to **SYNC**.

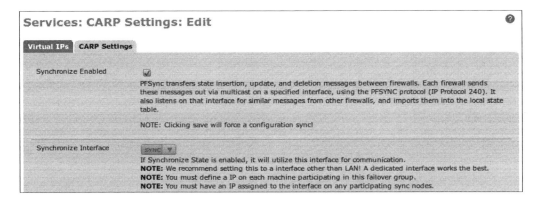

11. Check **Synchronize rules**:

12. Check **Synchronize nat**:

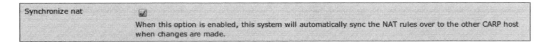

13. Check **Synchronize Virtual IPs**:

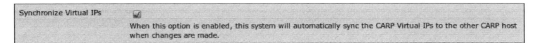

14. Set **Synchronize to IP** to the IP address of backup-pfsense.

15. Set **Remote System Password** to the password of backup-pfsense:

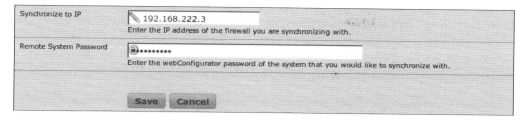

Synchronize to IP	192.168.222.3
	Enter the IP address of the firewall you are synchronizing with.
Remote System Password	•••••••••
	Enter the webConfigurator password of the system that you would like to synchronize with.

Save **Cancel**

16. **Save** the changes.

17. We must now configure a virtual IP address for the WAN interface on the primary-pfsense machine:

    1. Browse to **Firewall | Virtual IPs**.
    2. Click the **Virtual IPs** tab.
    3. Click the "plus" **button** to add a new virtual IP.
    4. Set the **Type** to **CARP**.
    5. Set the **Interface** to **WAN**.
    6. Set the **IP Address** to the single WAN address that will be used throughout your systems, regardless of whether the primary or backup firewall is in effect.
    7. Create a **Virtual IP Password**.
    8. Leave the **VHID Group** set to **1**.
    9. Leave the **Advertising Frequency** at **0**.
    10. Add a **Description**.

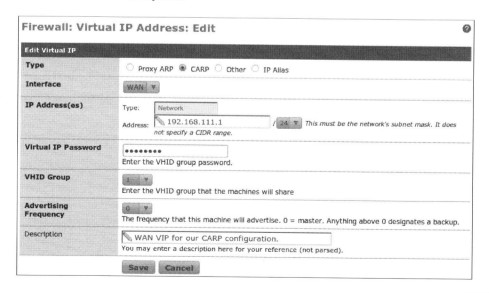

11. **Save** the changes.

12. **Apply** changes, if necessary.

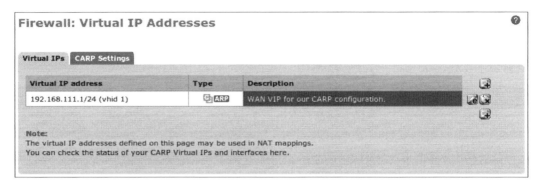

18. On the primary-pfsense machine we must now configure a virtual IP address for the LAN interface.

    1. Browse to **Firewall | Virtual IPs**.
    2. Click the **Virtual IPs** tab.
    3. Click the "plus" **button** to add a new virtual IP.
    4. Set the **Type** to **CARP**.
    5. Set the **Interface** to **LAN**.
    6. Set the **IP Address** to the single LAN address that will be used as the default gateway for all of our clients, regardless of whether the primary or backup firewall is in effect.
    7. Create a **Virtual IP Password**.
    8. Leave the **VHID Group** set to **2**.
    9. Leave the **Advertising Frequency** at **0**.
    10. Add a **Description**.

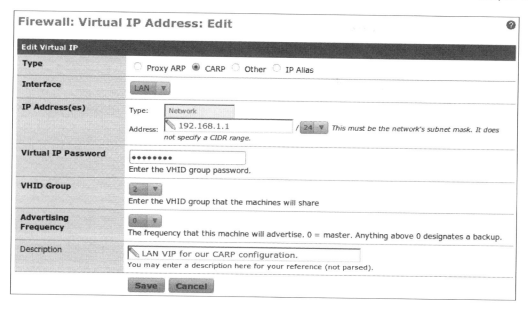

Firewall: Virtual IP Address: Edit

Edit Virtual IP

Type	○ Proxy ARP ◉ CARP ○ Other ○ IP Alias
Interface	LAN ▼
IP Address(es)	Type: Network Address: 192.168.1.1 / 24 ▼ *This must be the network's subnet mask. It does not specify a CIDR range.*
Virtual IP Password	•••••••• Enter the VHID group password.
VHID Group	2 ▼ Enter the VHID group that the machines will share
Advertising Frequency	0 ▼ The frequency that this machine will advertise. 0 = master. Anything above 0 designates a backup.
Description	LAN VIP for our CARP configuration. You may enter a description here for your reference (not parsed).

Save **Cancel**

11. **Save** the changes.

12. **Apply** changes, if necessary.

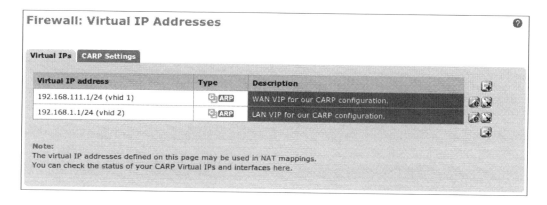

Firewall: Virtual IP Addresses

Virtual IPs **CARP Settings**

Virtual IP address	Type	Description	
192.168.111.1/24 (vhid 1)	ARP	WAN VIP for our CARP configuration.	
192.168.1.1/24 (vhid 2)	ARP	LAN VIP for our CARP configuration.	

Note:
The virtual IP addresses defined on this page may be used in NAT mappings.
You can check the status of your CARP Virtual IPs and interfaces here.

How it works...

This recipe has described how to create a failover firewall using CARP. The two firewalls constantly sync their rules, NAT, and virtual IP settings so that if the primary dies, the backup will seamlessly take its place.

The trick to synchronization is the advertising frequency set within each virtual IP. The primary server has an advertising frequency set to **0**, but when the settings are synchronized, the advertising frequency is incremented for the backup server (that is, the backup server's advertising frequency is set to **1**). That is how pfSense distinguishes the machines and synchronization settings.

See also

► The *Creating a NAT port forward rule* recipe in *Chapter 3, General Configuration*
► The *Creating a firewall rule* recipe in *Chapter 3, General Configuration*
► The *Creating a virtual IP* recipe in *Chapter 5, Advanced Configuration*

7
Services and Maintenance

In this chapter, we will cover:

- ▶ Enabling OLSR
- ▶ Enabling PPPoE
- ▶ Enabling RIP
- ▶ Enabling SNMP
- ▶ Enabling UPnP and NAT-PMP
- ▶ Enabling OpenNTPD
- ▶ Enabling **Wake On LAN** (**WOL**)
- ▶ Enabling SIPROXD
- ▶ Enabling external logging (syslog server)
- ▶ Using ping
- ▶ Using traceroute
- ▶ Backing up the configuration file
- ▶ Restoring the configuration file
- ▶ Configuring automatic configuration file backup
- ▶ Updating pfSense firmware

Introduction

pfSense offers a myriad of modern networking services and features. This chapter lays out the most commonly used services and maintenance features by describing what they do and how to use them.

The recipes in the first half of the chapter describe how to enable the most popular networking services in pfSense—everything from SNMP to logging. The *Using ping* and *Using traceroute* recipes describe how to use these indispensable networking tools, which are conveniently built into the pfSense web interface. The last several chapters describe the most essential of system services—backup, restore, and update.

Enabling OLSR

OLSR is an implementation of the **Optimized Link State Routing Protocol**, an IP routing protocol optimizing wireless mesh networks. A **mesh network** is a network consisting of two or more nodes, but what makes it unique is the way in which the nodes communicate with each other. The nodes have multiple routes across the network, improving reliability in the face of individual node failures.

This recipe describes how to enable **OLSR** (**Optimized Link State Routing**) in pfSense.

How to do it...

1. Browse to **Services | OLSR**.
2. Check **Enable OLSR**.
3. Choose an interface (*Ctrl* + click to select multiple interfaces).
4. **Save** the changes.

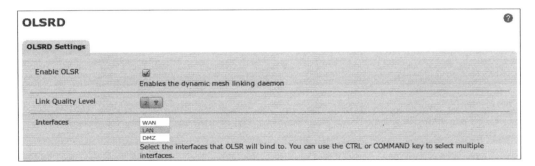

How it works...

pfSense's built-in support of OLSR allows configuration through the pfSense GUI. OLSR is highly scalable and highly portable, with an emphasis on reliability. OLSR is commonly used for mobile ad-hoc networks.

There's more...

Enabling the HTTPInfo plugin allows us to view and monitor the status of our OLSR mesh network:

1. Browse to **Services | OLSR**.
2. Check **Enable HTTPInfo Plugin**.
3. Specify an **HTTPInfo Port**.
4. Specify **Allowed Host(s)**.
5. Specify a subnet mask for **Allowed Host(s) Subnet**.
6. **Save** the changes.

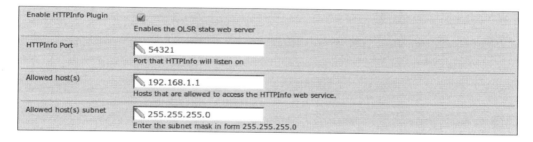

7. Browse to the HTTPInfo plugin site:

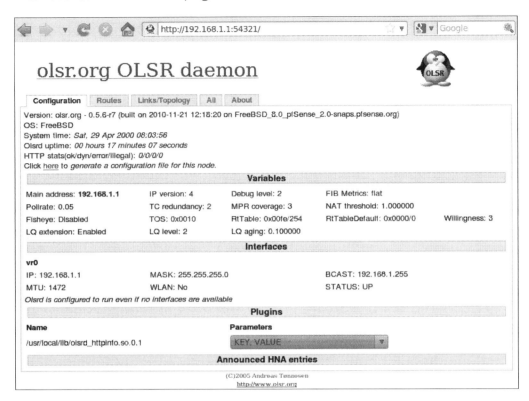

Enabling PPPoE

PPPoE stands for **Point-to-Point Protocol over Ethernet**, a network protocol that allows and encapsulates **Point-to-Point Protocol** (**PPP**) frames inside Ethernet frames. PPPoE allows two remote clients to connect and conveniently pass data between each other.

This recipe describes how to enable PPPoE on pfSense.

How to do it...

1. Browse to **Services | PPPoE Server**.
2. Click the "plus" button to add a new PPPoE instance.
3. Check **Enable PPPoE Server**.
4. Choose an **Interface**.
5. Choose a **Subnet Mask**.

6. Set **No. PPPoE Users** to the maximum number of clients we wish to allow.

7. Set **Server Address** to an unused IP address that pfSense will use to serve PPPoE clients.

8. Set **Remote Address Range** to the starting unused IP address. The range will run as far as the maximum number of PPPoE clients specified in step 6.

9. Add a **Description**.

10. Set **DNS Servers** to a particular set or leave them blank for defaults.

11. Add **User(s)**. Click the "plus" button to add a new user. Specify **Username**, **Password**, and **IP**.

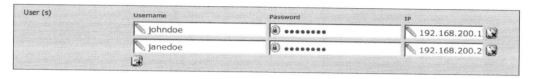

12. **Save** the changes.

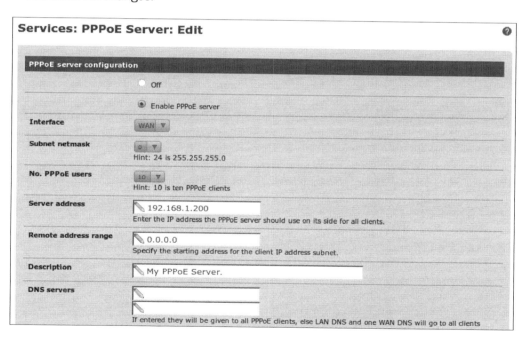

13. **Apply** changes, if necessary.

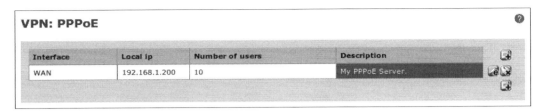

How it works...

The PPPoE service is generally used to fill the gap between PPP connections (dial-up) and Ethernet connections (broadband). Internet service providers often want to make use of their existing dial-up authentication systems on a broadband service and PPPoE allows them to do just that.

Enabling RIP

RIP stands for **Routing Information Protocol**, a dynamic routing protocol for local and wide area networks.

This recipe describes how to enable RIP in pfSense.

How to do it...

1. Browse to **Services | RIP**.
2. Check **Enable RIP**.
3. Select an interface (*Ctrl* + click to select multiple interfaces).
4. Select a **RIP Version**.
5. Set a **Password** if using RIP version 2.
6. **Save** the changes.

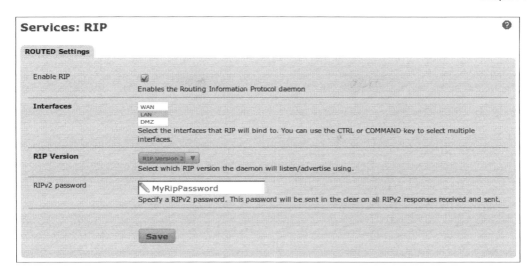

How it works...

The RIP protocol was the first dynamic routing protocol to be used in networks and was created for the purpose of sharing routing information between Unix hosts. The RIP protocol broadcasts the complete routing table on all active interfaces on a periodic basis (generally 30 seconds) and not surprisingly, more efficient routing protocols were quickly developed. Enabling the RIP service will allow administrators to support legacy hardware that may require it.

Enabling SNMP

SNMP stands for the **Simple Network Management Protocol**, a standard protocol enabling SNMP clients to query status information on machines that support SNMP.

This recipe describes how to enable the SNMP service in pfSense.

How to do it...

1. Browse to **Services | SNMP**.
2. Check **Enable SNMP Daemon**.
3. Leave **Polling Port** set to the default of UDP 161.
4. Specify a **System Location**.
5. Specify a **System Contact**.

6. Specify a **Read Community String**. The community string is roughly equivalent to a password and changing its value will ensure only authorized SNMP clients will be able to query the SNMP information from this machine.

 Be aware that SNMPv2 lacks encrypted connections.

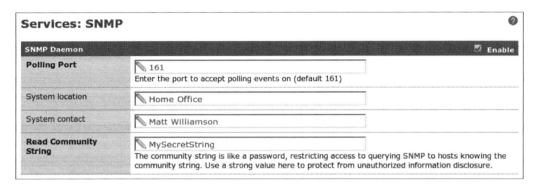

7. Select the **SNMP Modules** to be queried.

8. **Save** the changes.

How it works...

Enabling SNMP on pfSense will allow administrators to query vital system information from the SNMP client of their choice.

There's more...

SNMP traps are sent by SNMP-enabled devices (like pfSense) to specified servers when a significant event occurs. SNMP trap servers then decide how to process and handle the event, such as e-mailing a network administrator. SNMP traps are useful for network administrators who need to receive alerts quickly, rather than waiting for a potentially long polling cycle to detect any issues.

To specify an SNMP trap server in pfSense:

1. Browse to **Services | SNMP**.
2. Check **Enable SNMP Traps**.
3. Specify the **Trap Server Name**.
4. Specify the **Trap Server Port**.
5. Specify the **SNMP Trap String**.

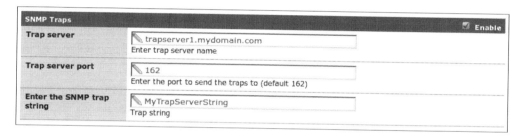

6. Save the changes.

See also

▶ PfSense SNMP Daemon documentation

`http://doc.pfsense.org/index.php/SNMP_Daemon`

Enabling UPnP and NAT-PMP

UPnP and NAT-PMP are simply different implementations of the same concept, automated NAT port mapping. These protocols are designed to allow clients to automatically configure the port-forwarding rules of a router/firewall. A common example is to enable UPnP so that an Xbox 360 can successfully connect to Xbox Live.

Generally, the UPnP protocol is used by Microsoft systems while the NAT-PMP is used by Apple systems.

This recipe describes how to enable UPnP and NAT-PMP in pfSense.

How to do it...

1. Browse to **Services | UPnP & NAT-PMP**.
2. Check **Enable UPnP & NAT-PMP**.
3. Check **Allow UPnP Port Mapping, Allow NAT-PMP Port Mapping**, or both.
4. Select the **Interface(s)** which will be applied (*Ctrl* + click to select multiple interfaces).

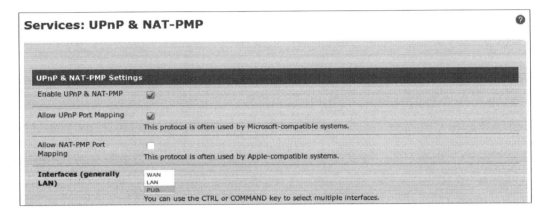

5. **Save** the changes.

How it works...

Enabling UPnP and NAT-PMP allows compatible devices to function properly on a given network without needing to define particular port-forwarding rules.

There's more...

The following optional features are available for the UPnP & NAT-PMP services in pfSense:

▶ Specify a **Maximum Download Speed** for UPnP and NAT-PMP devices

▶ Specify a **Maximum Upload Speed** for UPnP and NAT-PMP devices

▶ Specify to **Override the WAN Address** for UPnP and NAT-PMP devices

▶ Specify a particular **Traffic Shaping Queue** for UPnP and NAT-PMP clients

Maximum Download Speed (Kbits/second)	1500	
Maximum Upload Speed (Kbits/second)	500	
Override WAN address		
Traffic Shaping Queue		

- ▸ **Enable Log Packets** handled by UPnP and NAT-PMP clients
- ▸ Use **System Uptime** instead of UPnP and NAT-PMP service uptime
- ▸ By **Default Deny Access** to UPnP and NAT-PMP

- ▸ Define up to four **User specified permissions**

User specified permissions 1	
	Format: [allow or deny] [ext port or range] [int ipaddr or ipaddr/cdir] [int port or range] Example: allow 1024-65535 192.168.0.0/24 1024-65535
User specified permissions 2	
	Format: [allow or deny] [ext port or range] [int ipaddr or ipaddr/cdir] [int port or range]
User specified permissions 3	
	Format: [allow or deny] [ext port or range] [int ipaddr or ipaddr/cdir] [int port or range]
User specified permissions 4	
	Format: [allow or deny] [ext port or range] [int ipaddr or ipaddr/cdir] [int port or range]

Security warning

Allowing devices to make/modify their own firewall rules has some serious security implications. Microsoft's flagship firewall system ISA (and the newer TMG) refuses to even support these protocols. If you need to enable these services, please be aware of the risk. I would dedicate a separate interface for these services (and other risky traffic). You can see in the screenshots that I've only enabled UPnP for my PUB interface. This is an interface that I treat as very insecure, but it's useful for playing video games or allowing guests to surf the web freely.

See also

► PfSense UPnP Documentation

http://doc.pfsense.org/index.php/What_is_UPNP%3F

► Wikipedia UPnP Article

http://en.wikipedia.org/wiki/Universal_Plug_and_Play

► Wikipedia NAT-PMP Article

http://en.wikipedia.org/wiki/NAT_Port_Mapping_Protocol

Enabling OpenNTPD

The OpenNTPD service will serve date and time requests to clients that request them. This recipe describes how to enable the OpenNTPD service in pfSense.

How to do it...

1. Browse to **Services | OpenNTPD**.
2. Check **Enable** to enable the NTP daemon service.
3. Select the interface(s) the NTP daemon service will listen on.

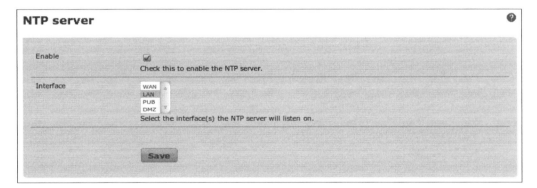

4. **Save** the changes.

How it works...

OpenNTPD is an open-source implementation of the Network Time Protocol service. Devices within your network can now query the pfSense firewall with NTP and receive accurate time data from it.

Client machines can take a few hours to become fully synchronized with the OpenNTPD service. Be patient.

See also

▸ PfSense NTPD Documentation

  http://doc.pfsense.org/index.php/NTP_Server_%28OpenNTPD%29

▸ OpenNTPD.org

  http://www.openntpd.org/

▸ Wikipedia OpenNTPD Article

  http://en.wikipedia.org/wiki/OpenNTPD

Enabling Wake On LAN (WOL)

pfSense can send a **Wake-on-LAN** packet (also known as a **magic packet**) to a compatible device to "wake it up" out of suspended/sleep mode. This recipe describes how to use the Wake-on-LAN facility in pfSense.

How to do it...

1. Browse to **Services | Wake on LAN**.
2. Select the **Interface** which contains the device we'd like to wake up.
3. Enter the device's **MAC address**.

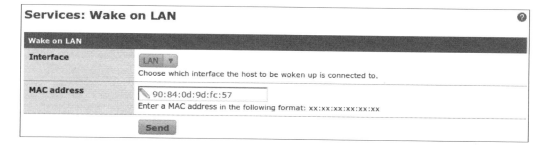

4. Click **Send**.

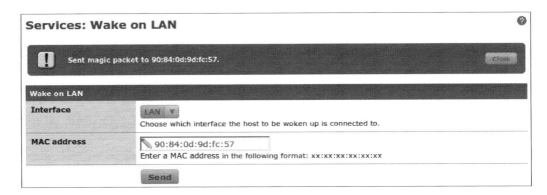

How it works...

The Wake-on-LAN service can send "magic packets" to any network devices that support and are properly configured for Wake on LAN. When a properly configured device receives a magic packet, it will "wake the machine up" out of sleep or standby mode.

 Note that on older hardware, properly configuring an NIC can involve attaching a special WOL cable to the motherboard and then enabling WOL in that machine's BIOS.

There's more...

You can store the MAC addresses of any machines that support Wake on LAN:

1. Browse to **Services | Wake on LAN**.
2. Click the "plus" button to add a WOL Mac Address entry.
3. Select the **Interface** that contains the device.
4. Specify the device's **MAC address**.
5. Add a **Description**.

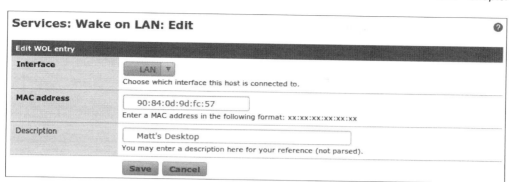

6. **Save** the changes.

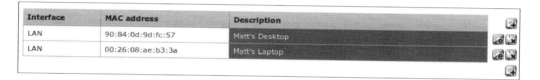

7. Click the **MAC address** of any of the stored clients to send a magic packet.

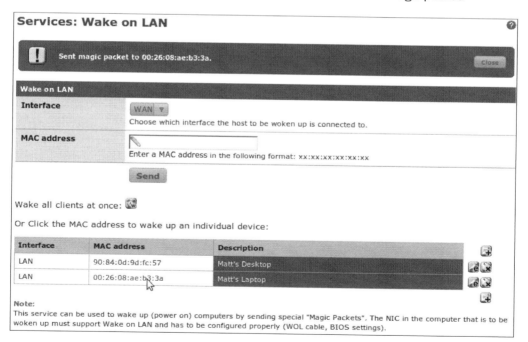

Wake All

Instead of waking clients individually, there may be times when we want to wake them all up at once—simply click the **Wake All** button.

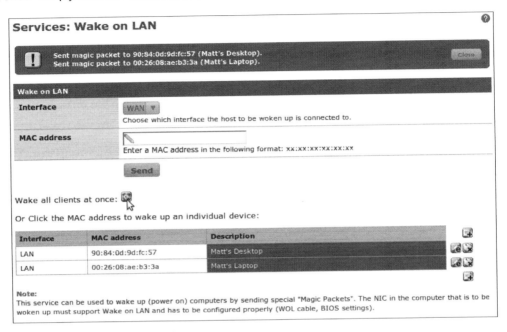

See also

▶ PfSense Wake-on-LAN Documentation

```
http://doc.pfsense.org/index.php/Wake_on_LAN
```

▶ Wikipedia Wake-on-LAN Article

```
http://en.wikipedia.org/wiki/Wake-on-LAN
```

Enabling external logging (syslog server)

Syslog is a standardized system for logging all types of information. Syslog client and server implementations exist for all major operating systems.

Most Linux distributions are already running the syslog service, so setting up a centralized server is only a matter of deciding which machine to use, configuring that machine to listen for syslog data on the network, and then configuring all other machines to direct syslog messages to that server.

This recipe describes how to configure pfSense to write logs to an external syslog server.

Getting ready

To turn a Windows machine into a centralized syslog server, take a look at the Kiwi Syslog Server and Log Viewer.

How to do it...

1. Browse to **Status | System Logs**.
2. Click the **Settings** tab.
3. Check **Enable syslog'ing to remote syslog server**.
4. Specify the IP addresses of up to three remote syslog servers.
5. Check **Everything** to record all messages or select specific events.

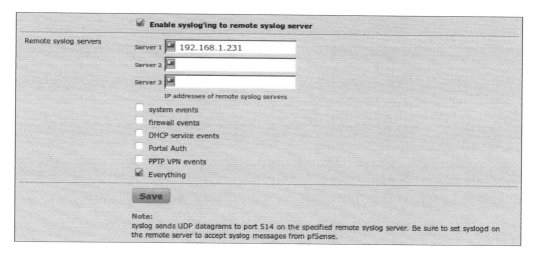

6. **Save** the changes.

How it works...

By writing logs to an external syslog server, we have taken significant weight off the resources of our pfSense machine. This can have a very positive effect on many pfSense boxes that are light on memory and hard drive space, and is especially useful for machines using limited-lifetime disks such as CompactFlash drives.

There's more...

If you are *not* configuring an external syslog server, the following internal logging options are available in pfSense:

► Show log entries in reverse order (newest entries on top)

► Number of log entries to show

► Log packets blocked by the default rule

► Show raw filter logs

► Disable writing log files to the local RAM disk

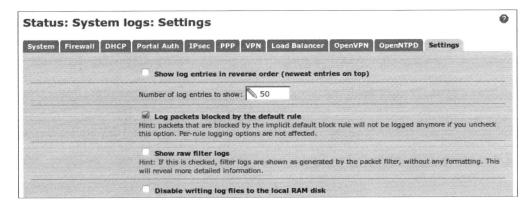

See also

► PfSense Log Settings Documentation

http://doc.pfsense.org/index.php/Log_Settings

► Wikipedia Syslog Article

http://en.wikipedia.org/wiki/Syslog

► Kiwi Syslog Server and Log Viewer

http://www.kiwisyslog.com/

Using ping

pfSense exposes the ping service that's included on almost all operating systems. This can be handy for administrators since pfSense can ping on any machine from any specified interface. This recipe describes how to use the ping service in pfSense.

How to do it...

1. Browse to **Diagnostics | Ping**.
2. Set **Host** to the IP Address or hostname of the machine we're trying to ping.
3. Choose the **Interface** to initiate the ping from.
4. Select a **Count**, the default of 3 is generally adequate.

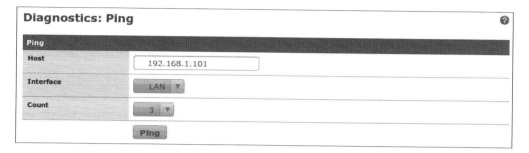

5. Press the **Ping** button.

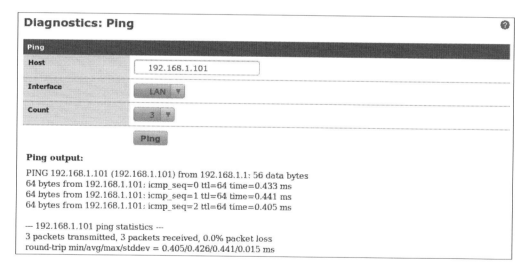

How it works...

The ping utility allows administrators to ping any machine on any interface, *from* any interface. Ping is an indispensable tool and having it built into the firewall's web interface is a great tool for administrators.

See also

▶ PfSense Ping Host Documentation

`http://doc.pfsense.org/index.php/Ping_Host`

▶ Wikipedia Ping Article

`http://en.wikipedia.org/wiki/Ping`

Using traceroute

.pfSense exposes the traceroute service that's included on almost all operating systems. This can be handy for administrators who need to perform an ad-hoc traceroute.

This recipe describes how to use the traceroute utility in pfSense.

How to do it...

1. Browse to **Diagnostics | Traceroute**.
2. Set **Host** to the IP Address or hostname of the machine we're trying to trace.
3. Choose the **Maximum number of hops** for the trace to jump.
4. Optionally check **Use ICMP**.

5. Click the **Traceroute** button.

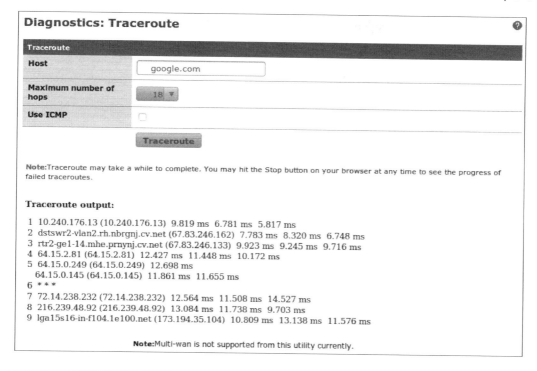

Diagnostics: Traceroute

Traceroute

Host	google.com
Maximum number of hops	18 ▼
Use ICMP	☐

Traceroute

Note:Traceroute may take a while to complete. You may hit the Stop button on your browser at any time to see the progress of failed traceroutes.

Traceroute output:

```
 1  10.240.176.13 (10.240.176.13)  9.819 ms  6.781 ms  5.817 ms
 2  dstswr2-vlan2.rh.nbrgnj.cv.net (67.83.246.162)  7.783 ms  8.320 ms  6.748 ms
 3  rtr2-ge1-14.mhe.prnynj.cv.net (67.83.246.133)  9.923 ms  9.245 ms  9.716 ms
 4  64.15.2.81 (64.15.2.81)  12.427 ms  11.448 ms  10.172 ms
 5  64.15.0.249 (64.15.0.249)  12.698 ms
    64.15.0.145 (64.15.0.145)  11.861 ms  11.655 ms
 6  * * *
 7  72.14.238.232 (72.14.238.232)  12.564 ms  11.508 ms  14.527 ms
 8  216.239.48.92 (216.239.48.92)  13.084 ms  11.738 ms  9.703 ms
 9  lga15s16-in-f104.1e100.net (173.194.35.104)  10.809 ms  13.138 ms  11.576 ms
```

Note: Multi-wan is not supported from this utility currently.

How it works...

The traceroute utility allows administrators to perform an ad-hoc trace directly from the pfSense web interface.

> Traceroute can sometimes take a long time to complete. Click the browser's stop button at any time to cancel the traceroute and display the results.

See also

▶ pfSense Traceroute Documentation

http://doc.pfsense.org/index.php/Traceroute

▶ Wikipedia Traceroute Article

http://en.wikipedia.org/wiki/Traceroute

Backing up the configuration file

Backing up configuration files is an essential part of any administrator's position. This recipe describes how to back up the pfSense configuration file.

Getting ready...

pfSense configuration files are stored in a plain-text XML format by default, but it also gives you an option to encrypt them.

How to do it...

1. Browse to **Diagnostics | Backup/restore**.
2. Select the **Backup/Restore** tab.
3. Set the **Backup area** to **ALL**. For a list of all available areas, see the following *Backup areas* section.
4. Leave **Do not backup package information** unchecked.
5. Leave **Do not backup RRD data** checked.

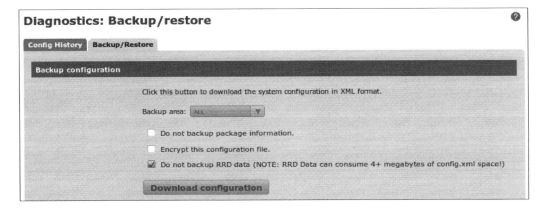

6. Click **Download configuration**.
7. **Save** the file to a secure location.

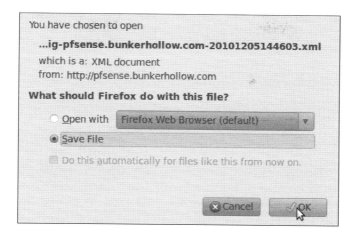

How it works...

pfSense allows an administrator to download the entire pfSense configuration in a single XML file to any local or networked drive.

There's more...

Some passwords will be stored in plain text! If this is a concern, be sure to check the **Encrypt this configuration file** option and specify a password.

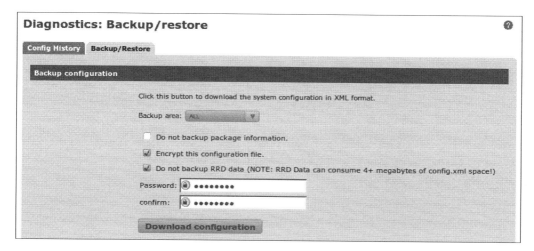

Backup areas

Currently in pfSense 2.0, the following backup areas are available:

 ▸ ALL
 ▸ Aliases
 ▸ DNS Forwarder
 ▸ DHCP Server
 ▸ Firewall Rules
 ▸ Interface
 ▸ IPSec
 ▸ NAT
 ▸ Package Manager
 ▸ PPTP Server
 ▸ Scheduled Tasks
 ▸ Syslog
 ▸ System
 ▸ System Tunables
 ▸ SNMP Server

See also

 ▸ PfSense Configuration Backup/Restore Documentation

   ```
   http://doc.pfsense.org/index.php/Configuration_Backup_and_
   Restore
   ```

Restoring the configuration file

This recipe describes how to restore the pfSense configuration file.

Getting ready...

Restoring configuration files is an essential part of any administrator's position. pfSense configuration files are stored in a plain-text XML format by default, but an encryption option is available.

How to do it...

1. Browse to **Diagnostics | Backup/restore**.

2. Select the **Backup/Restore** tab.

3. Set the **Restore area** to **ALL**. For a list of all available areas, see the following *Restore areas* section:

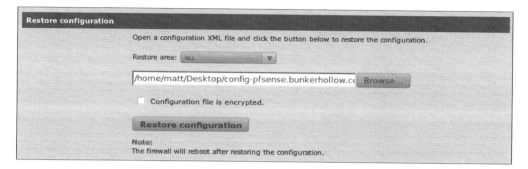

4. Click **Restore configuration** and pfSense will reboot.

How it works...

pfSense allows an administrator to restore the entire pfSense configuration from a single XML file.

There's more...

If the configuration file was encrypted, be sure to check the **Configuration file is encrypted** option and specify the correct password:

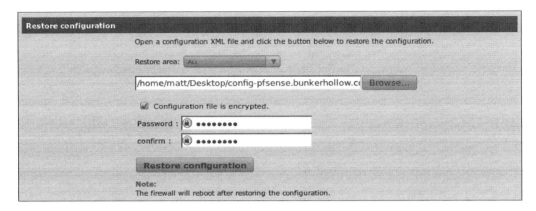

Restore areas

Currently in pfSense 2.0 the following back up areas are available:

- ALL
- Aliases
- Captive Portal
- Captive Portal Vouchers
- DNS Forwarder
- DHCP Server
- Firewall Rules
- Interface
- IPSec
- NAT
- OpenVPN
- Package Manager
- PPTP Server
- Scheduled Tasks
- Static Routes
- Syslog
- System

- ▸ System Tunables
- ▸ SNMP Server
- ▸ Traffic Shaper
- ▸ VLANs
- ▸ Wake on LAN

See also

- ▸ PfSense Configuration Backup/Restore Documentation

  `http://doc.pfsense.org/index.php/Configuration_Backup_and_Restore`

Configuring automatic configuration file backup

This recipe describes how to configure pfSense to automatically back up its configuration file.

Getting ready

Users with a pfSense support subscription can configure automated backup to external pfSense servers using their `portal.pfsense.org` login credentials. Currently, only paid support subscribers have access to this feature.

How to do it...

1. Browse to **Diagnostics | AutoConfigBackup**.
2. Click the **Settings** tab.
3. Enter our **Subscription Username**.
4. Enter our **Subscription Password**.
5. Confirm **Subscription Password**.
6. Enter our **Encryption Password**.

7. Confirm **Encryption Password**.

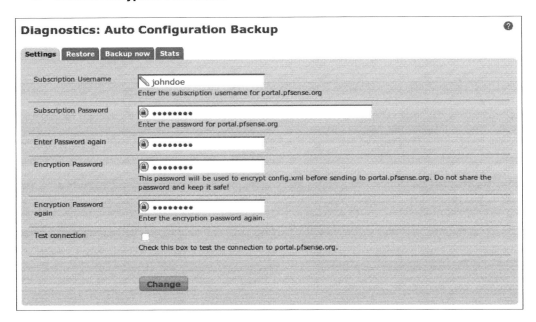

8. **Save** the changes.

How it works...

Automated backups can now be securely stored on a set of external pfSense servers. This is convenient for users to have a safe external backup location, as well as for support staff, which will be able to track configuration changes while troubleshooting issues.

There's more...

A pfSense support subscription makes automated backup available. Also, restores can be done directly from the pfSense servers and backup/restore statistics are available directly from the **Stats** tab.

See also

▶ pfSense Automated Configuration Backup Documentation

  http://doc.pfsense.org/index.php/AutoConfigBackup

▶ pfSense Premium Portal

  https://portal.pfsense.org/

Updating pfSense firmware

This recipe describes how to update the pfSense firmware.

Getting ready

Let's be sure to make a backup of our current configuration file before we proceed with a complete system upgrade.

How to do it...

1. Browse to **System | Firmware**.
2. Click the **Auto Update tab**.
3. Click **Invoke Auto Upgrade**.

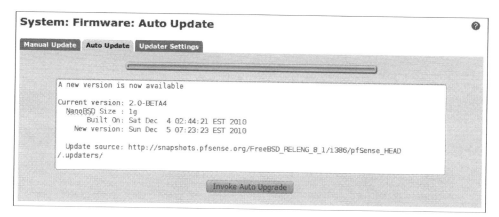

4. Observe the download status.

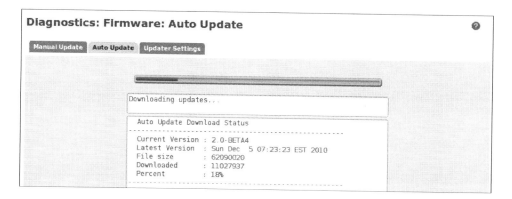

5. Once the download is complete, pfSense will upgrade itself and reboot.

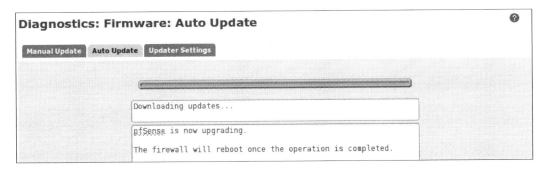

6. On the first login after the system has rebooted, we'll be redirected to **Package Manager** status page.

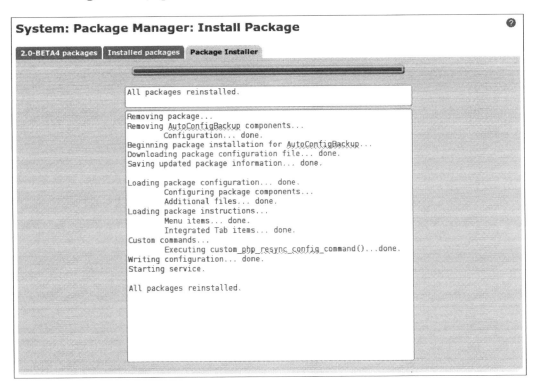

How it works...

pfSense will contact a web service at `http://pfsense.org/` to determine the latest firmware version, and to download that firmware if needed.

There's more...

pfSense also allows for a manual firmware upgrade, outlined in the steps below:

1. Download the appropriate version from `http://pfsense.org/` and save it locally.

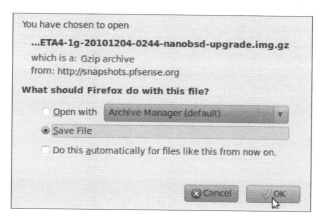

2. Browse to **System | Firmware**.
3. Click the **Manual Update tab**.

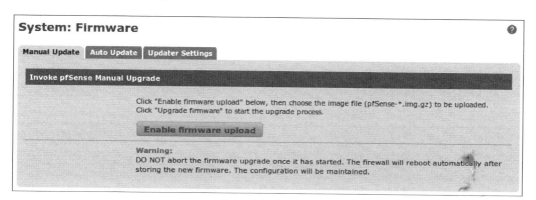

4. Click the **Enable firmware upload** button.

5. Click **Browse** to locate the firmware file we've downloaded.

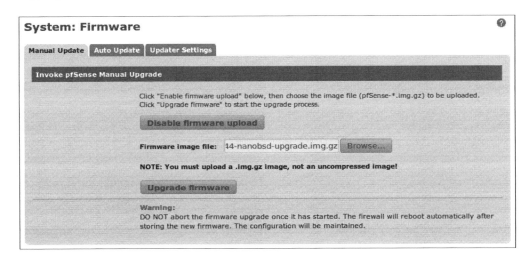

6. Click **Upgrade firmware**.

Upgrade in progress

Any attempt to access the pfSense web interface while an upgrade is in progress will redirect us to the following page and animation. Once the upgrade is complete, the machine will reboot.

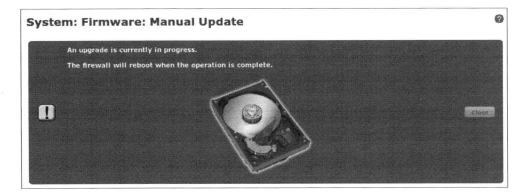

System Dashboard shortcut

If a new version of pfSense is available, an **Update available** notification will be displayed on the **Status Dashboard** homepage in the **Version** section of **System Information**.

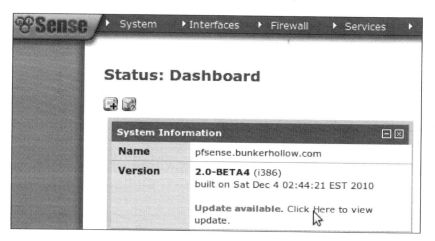

See also

▶ The *Backing up the configuration file* recipe

▶ pfSense Firmware Update Documentation

http://doc.pfsense.org/index.php/Firmware_Updates

Monitoring and Logging

In this chapter, we will cover:

- Customizing the Status Dashboard
- Monitoring current traffic
- Configuring SMTP e-mail notifications
- Viewing system logs
- Configuring an external syslog server
- Viewing RRD graphs
- Viewing DHCP leases
- Monitoring the packet filter with pfInfo
- Monitoring traffic with pfTop
- Monitoring system activity

Introduction

Once pfSense is up and running, it's important to understand how to properly monitor the system. Learning to use the status monitor and logging tools built into pfSense will make an administrator's life all the much easier. The following recipes describe how to monitor and log the majority of features available within pfSense.

Customizing the Status Dashboard

This recipe describes how to personally configure the **Status Dashboard**.

How to do it...

1. Browse to **Status | Dashboard**.

2. Click the "plus" button to add a widget:

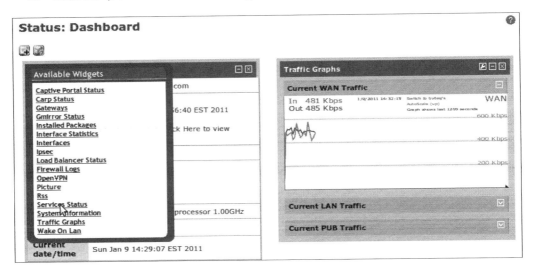

3. Click the wrench button to configure settings for a particular widget.

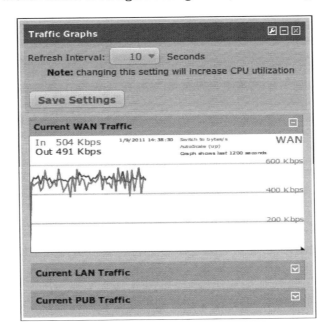

4. Click the "minimize" button to collapse a widget, or the "close" button to remove one from the screen.

5. Drag and drop widgets by their title to change their position on the screen.

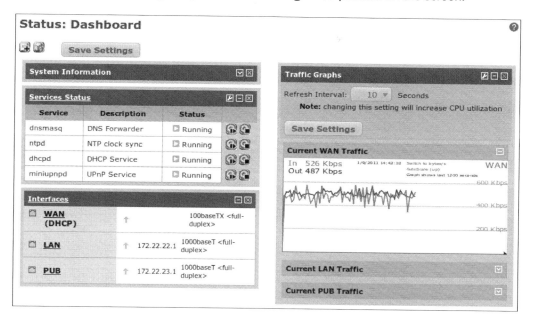

6. **Save** the settings.

7. **Apply** changes, if necessary.

How it works...

The **Status Dashboard** is among the many new features added to pfSense 2.0. By customizing the dashboard to display the information you are interested in, administration becomes much easier. If properly configured, the dashboard may be the only page an administrator may need to visit to accomplish many common tasks.

There's more...

Many of the widgets available on the dashboard also have a corresponding status item that can be found in the **Status** drop-down menu.

Monitoring current traffic

This recipe describes how to monitor current incoming and outgoing traffic in pfSense.

How to do it...

1. Browse to **Status | Traffic Graph**.
2. Select an **Interface** to monitor.

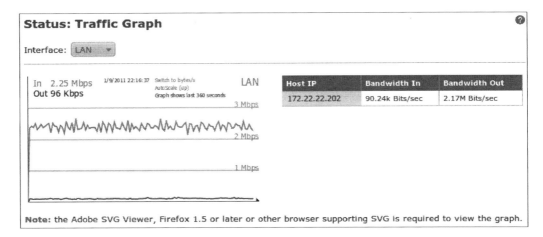

How it works...

The traffic graph shows real-time information of all traffic flowing to and from a particular interface. The table to the right will show the traffic information for the top few devices on the network.

 Your browser must support SVG graphics, as Firefox does. If your browser doesn't support SVG graphics, install the Adobe SVG Viewer.

See also

▸ pfSense Traffic Graph Documentation

   `http://doc.pfsense.org/index.php/Traffic_Graph`

▸ Adobe SVG Viewer

   `http://www.adobe.com/svg/viewer/install/`

Configuring SMTP e-mail notifications

This recipe describes how to configure SMTP settings to send notification e-mails.

Getting ready

Sending e-mails from pfSense requires access to an SMTP server

How to do it...

1. Browse to **System | Advanced**.
2. Click the **Notifications** tab.
3. Enter the **IP Address of the E-Mail server**.
4. Enter the **SMTP Port of the E-Mail server**.
5. Enter the **From e-Mail address**.
6. Enter the **Notification E-Mail address**.
7. Enter the **Notification E-Mail auth username**.
8. Enter the **Notification E-Mail auth password**.

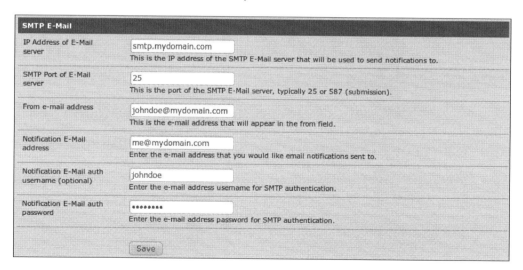

9. **Save** the changes.
10. **Apply** changes, if necessary.

How it works...

pfSense will send an e-mail notification using the information supplied to notify administrators of significant system events.

There's more...

Once our settings are saved, a test e-mail will be sent automatically. If you do not receive the test e-mail, check the system logs for more information. Browse to the **Status | System Logs | System** tab and look for any e-mail-related log entries:

Viewing system logs

This recipe describes how to view the pfSense system logs.

How to do it...

1. Browse to **Status | System logs**.
2. Click the **Settings** tab.
3. Check **Show log entries in reverse order (newest entries on top)**.
4. **Save** the changes.
5. Click the **DHCP** tab (for example) to view the most recent DHCP events:

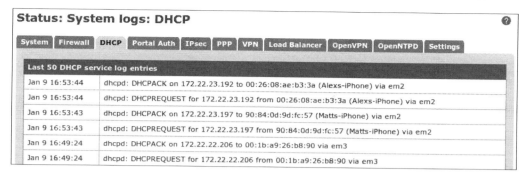

How it works...

pfSense records significant events and logs them internally. The **System logs** menu item allows us to view the logs to help troubleshoot a variety of administrative issues.

The following sections describe how configure the alternate log views provided for firewall events.

There's more...

Logging information is gathered and displayed for the following services:

- ► System
- ► Firewall
- ► DHCP
- ► Portal Auth
- ► IPSec
- ► PPP
- ► VPN
- ► Load Balancer
- ► OpenVPN
- ► OpenNTPD

 If logging on to an external syslog server, there won't be any data on these pages.

Firewall log: Normal View

The following is a screenshot of the normal firewall log view:

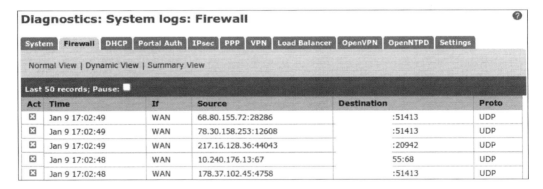

Firewall log: Dynamic View

The following is a screenshot of the dynamic firewall log view:

Firewall log: Summary View

The following is a screenshot of the summary firewall log view:

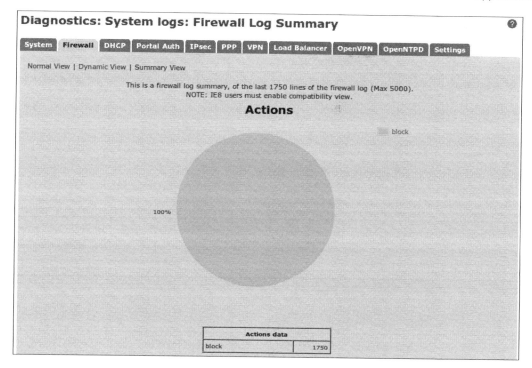

See also

> ▸ The *Configuring an external syslog server* recipe

Configuring an external syslog server

This recipe describes how to configure pfSense to use an external logging server.

Getting ready

To configure pfSense to use a separate server for logging, we obviously need a separate logging server to accomplish this. The following sections describe how to create a syslog server on each of the major operating systems.

How to do it...

1. Browse to **Status | System Logs**.
2. Click the **Settings** tab.
3. Check **Enable syslog'ing to remote syslog server**.
4. Enter the IP address(es) of our external syslog servers.
5. Check the types of events to be logged.

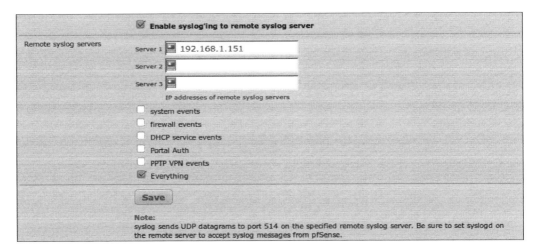

6. **Save** the changes.
7. **Apply** changes, if necessary.

How it works...

Once configured, pfSense will send event logs to an external server instead of logging them locally. This is a great way to free up resources on a pfSense machine and to save larger and more detailed logs to a machine with much more disk space.

Running a syslog service in Linux/Mac OS

Almost all Linux and Mac OS distributions already include the **syslogd** service. Visit the following page for more information: http://linux.die.net/man/8/syslogd.

Running a syslog service in Windows

Download and install the Kiwi Syslog Server for Windows from http://www.kiwisyslog.com.

See also

- ▸ The *Viewing system logs* recipe
- ▸ Linux syslogd documentation
  http://linux.die.net/man/8/syslogd
- ▸ Kiwi Syslog Server
  http://www.kiwisyslog.com

Viewing RRD graphs

This recipe describes how to view RRD graphs from within pfSense.

How to do it...

1. Browse to **Status | RRD Graphs**.
2. Choose the **System** tab.
3. Select the **Graphs**, **Style**, and **Period** of the data we'd like displayed.

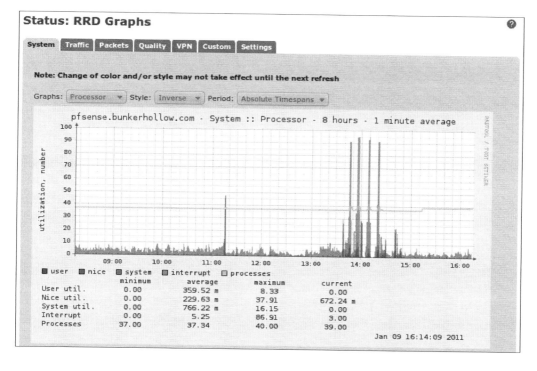

How it works...

pfSense records system data and uses the open-source RRD toolset to present that data graphically. Analyzing system data with the RRD graphs is a great way to monitor and troubleshoot all sorts of administrative issues.

pfSense can analyze and display the following information in RRD graph format.

System

The **System** tab gathers and displays hardware load information.

- ▶ Throughput
- ▶ States
- ▶ Process
- ▶ Memory
- ▶ All

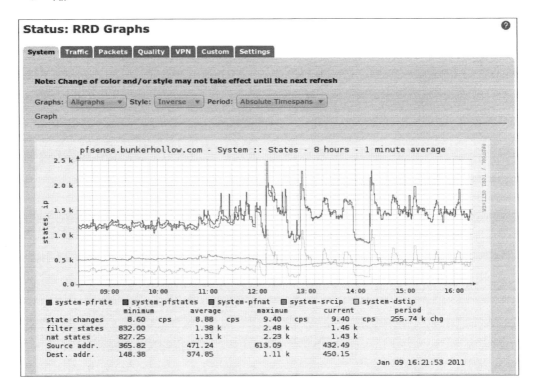

Traffic

The **Traffic** tab gathers and displays network throughput information for each of the systems interfaces.

- ▸ Outbound
- ▸ WAN
- ▸ LAN
- ▸ Optional Interface(s)
- ▸ OpenVPN
- ▸ IPSec
- ▸ All

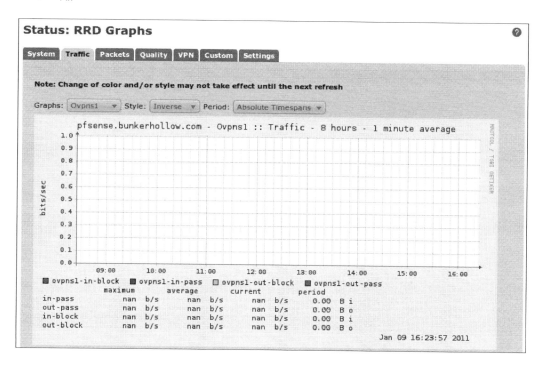

Packets

The **Packets** tab gathers and displays packet throughput information for each of the systems interfaces.

- ▶ Outbound
- ▶ WAN
- ▶ LAN
- ▶ Optional Interface(s)
- ▶ OpenVPN
- ▶ IPSec
- ▶ All

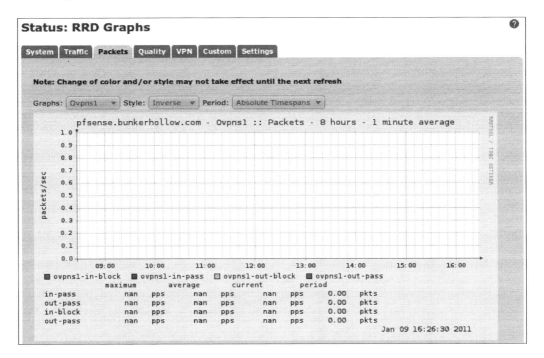

Quality

The **Quality** tab gathers and displays packet loss information for each of the systems interfaces.

- ▶ Outbound
- ▶ WAN
- ▶ Gateway(s)
- ▶ All

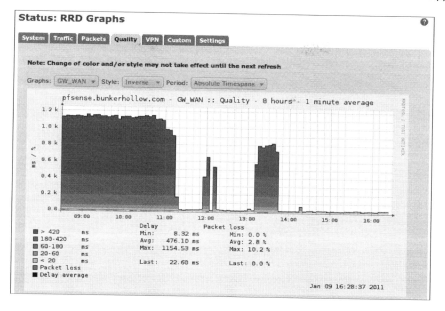

VPN

The **VPN** tab gathers and display VPN throughput information (if applicable).

- ▸ OpenVPN
- ▸ IPSec
- ▸ PPTP
- ▸ All

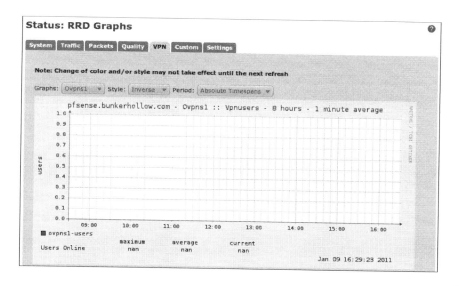

Custom

Choose any previous graph and specify starting and ending timestamps.

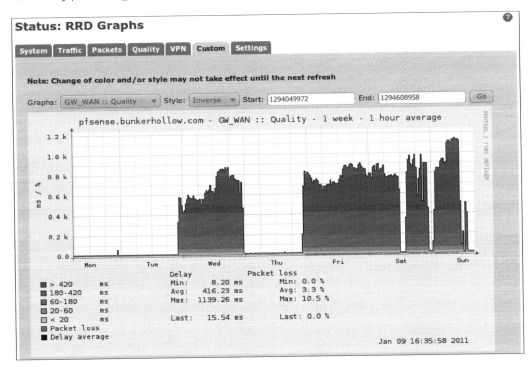

See also

▶   RRDTool

http://www.mrtg.org/rrdtool/

Viewing DHCP leases

This recipe describes how to view DHCP leases served by pfSense.

How to do it...

1.   Browse to **Status | DHCP leases**:

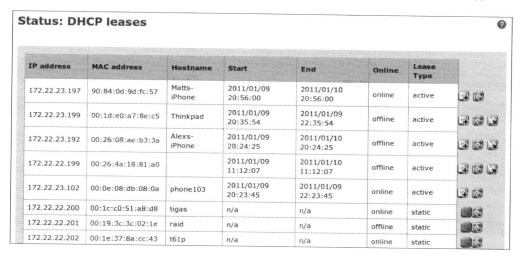

2. By default, only **active** and **static** leases are shown. To view **expired** leases, click the **Show all configured leases** button:

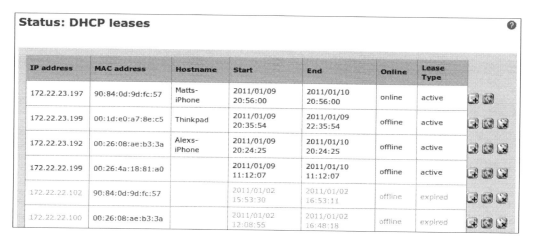

How it works...

When configured as a DHCP server, pfSense hands out an IP address to any device that requests one. This page is often the first page to check when troubleshooting network connectivity problems with a device.

Adding a static DHCP mapping

If we see a device on the list that'd we'd always like to have the same IP address, we can add a static mapping for it by simply clicking the "plus" button.

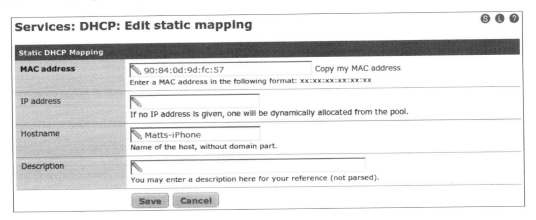

Sending a wake on LAN mapping

If we see a device that we want to send "magic packets" to, we can add a WOL mapping by simply clicking the **w** button:

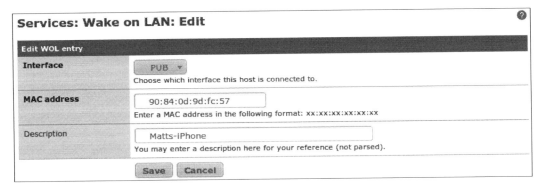

See also

▶   The *Creating static DHCP mappings* recipe in *Chapter 2, Essential Services*

Managing services

This recipe describes how to manage the services running in pfSense.

How to do it...

1. Browse to **Status | Services**:

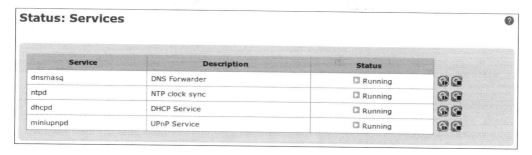

2. To restart a service, click the **restart** button:

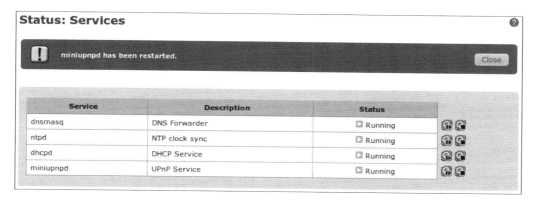

3. To stop a service, click the **stop** button:

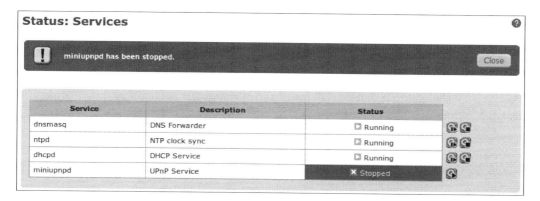

4. To start a service, click the **start** button:

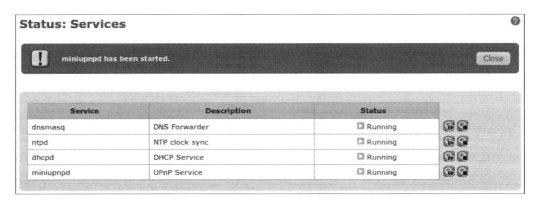

How it works...

pfSense package management allows for services to be independently stopped and started. This is particularly helpful to administrators who can force a service to restart without taking down the entire system.

See also

▸   pfSense Service Status Documentation

http://doc.pfsense.org/index.php/Services_Status

Monitoring the packet filter with pfInfo

This recipe describes how to view pfSense's packet filter information.

How to do it...

1. Browse to **Diagnostics | pfInfo**:

Diagnostics: pfInfo

```
Status: Enabled for 7 days 07:02:29          Debug: Urgent

Hostid:    0xd54c9328
Checksum: 0x09f3c370c92d212bc6f153a78f8c73f6

Interface Stats for em2                IPv4                IPv6
   Bytes In                         45587928                  0
   Bytes Out                       247865172                 96
   Packets In
      Passed                         230792                  0
      Blocked                           402                  0
   Packets Out
      Passed                         598572                  0
      Blocked                             0                  1

State Table                          Total                Rate
   current entries                    2770
   searches                        467273767            741.5/s
   inserts                           3144108              5.0/s
   removals                          3141338              5.0/s
Source Tracking Table
   current entries                        0
   searches                               0              0.0/s
   inserts                                0              0.0/s
   removals                               0              0.0/s
Counters
   match                            3966931              6.3/s
```

How it works...

System administrators will find the following information displayed about the packet filter:

- ▸ Interface statistics
- ▸ State table statistics
- ▸ Limits configuration
- ▸ Rule state
- ▸ Byte counters

See also

- ▸ PfSense pfInfo Documentation

  http://doc.pfsense.org/index.php/Packet_Filter_Information

Monitoring traffic with pfTop

This recipe describes how to view the current traffic flow using the pfTop utility.

How to do it...

1. Browse to **Diagnostics | pfTop**:

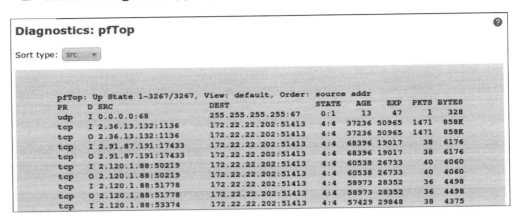

How it works...

System administrators can use the **pfTop** utility to monitor current bandwidth and traffic. The data displayed by this utility can be sorted by any of the following criteria:

- ▸ Bytes
- ▸ Age
- ▸ Destination
- ▸ Destination Port
- ▸ Expiration
- ▸ None
- ▸ Peak
- ▸ Packets
- ▸ Rate
- ▸ Size
- ▸ Source Port
- ▸ Source

See also

▸ pfSense Bandwidth Monitoring Documentation

```
http://doc.pfsense.org/index.php/How_can_I_monitor_bandwidth_
usage%3F#pftop
```

Monitoring system activity

This recipe describes how to monitor system activity in pfSense.

How to do it...

1. Browse to **Diagnostics | System Activity**:

Diagnostics: System Activity

```
last pid:  6410;  load averages:  0.14,   0.27,   0.16  up 7+07:24:08      22:03:31
106 processes: 2 running, 80 sleeping, 24 waiting

Mem: 45M Active, 41M Inact, 68M Wired, 396K Cache, 110M Buf, 827M Free
Swap:


  PID USERNAME PRI NICE   SIZE    RES STATE    TIME    WCPU COMMAND
   10 root     171 ki31    0K     8K RUN    166.3H 92.97% idle
   11 root     -68    -     0K   192K WAIT   178:51  0.98% {irq20: fxp0}
   11 root     -68    -     0K   192K WAIT   151:35  0.98% {irq265: em3:rx 0}
22730 root      48    0 54692K 15836K piperd   0:11  0.98% php
   11 root     -68    -     0K   192K WAIT    12:19  0.00% {irq266: em3:tx 0}
   11 root     -32    -     0K   192K WAIT    12:18  0.00% {swi4: clock}
   11 root     -64    -     0K   192K WAIT    10:50  0.00% {irq15: ata1}
   13 root     -16    -     0K     8K -       10:13  0.00% yarrow
31177 root      44    0  3316K  1300K select   3:33  0.00% apinger
10765 root      76   20  3656K  1424K wait     3:22  0.00% sh
19205 root      44    0  3316K   888K piperd   3:14  0.00% logger
53022 nobody    44    0  5552K  2496K select   1:43  0.00% dnsmasq
12723 root      76    0 54692K 16456K accept   1:15  0.00% php
18890 root      44    0 11032K  8280K bpf      1:12  0.00% tcpdump
    0 root     -16    0    0K   112K sched     0:54  0.00% {swapper}
52249 dhcpd     44    0  7776K  4068K select    0:52  0.00% dhcpd
    2 root      -8    -    0K     8K -         0:47  0.00% g_event
    7 root     -16    -    0K     8K pftm      0:45  0.00% pfpurge
```

How it works...

Administrators can monitor the core system activity of pfSense, including the following resources:

- ▶ Last process ID (PID)
- ▶ Load averages
- ▶ Uptime
- ▶ Process statistics
- ▶ Memory statistics
- ▶ Swap statistics

See also

- ▶ pfSense System Activity Documentation

    http://doc.pfsense.org/index.php/System_Activity

B
Determining our Hardware Requirements

This appendix covers the following topics:

- ▶ Determining our deployment scenario
- ▶ Determining our throughput requirements
- ▶ Determining our interface requirements
- ▶ Choosing the standard or embedded image
- ▶ Choosing a form factor

Introduction

Whether our environment is a home network consisting of two computers or a corporate data center comprised of hundreds of machines, it's essential to begin by determining exactly what we need from our firewall.

The versatility of pfSense presents us with a wide array of configuration options which, compared to other offerings, makes determining requirements a little more difficult and that much more important. The latest firewall product from Microsoft, for example, requires a dual-core processor, 2 GB of RAM, 2.5 GB of hard disk space, and the latest version of the Windows Server platform. In this case, we'd probably end up buying a new server, and that would be fine. We would be finished with our decision and we wouldn't need to read this chapter.

pfSense would run just fine on new hardware but as we'll see, pfSense offers numerous other alternatives to fit any environment's security needs.

Determining our deployment scenario

This recipe will determine which of the many pfSense deployment scenarios is right for our environment by analyzing our network diagram.

Getting ready

This recipe requires the use of our network diagram to understand how and where pfSense will fit into our environment. As an example we'll be using my own home network diagram. This diagram is a good example of a typical small-office environment (minus the video game consoles).

How to do it...

1. Let's analyze our network diagram:

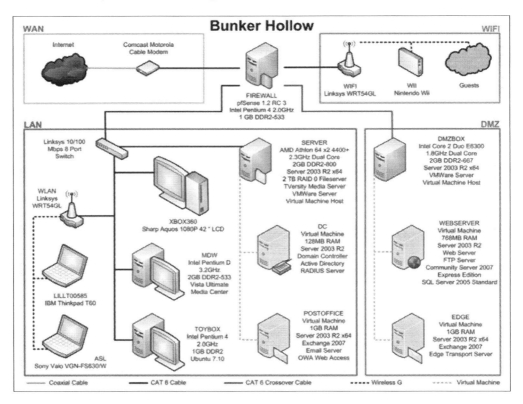

2. In this small-office scenario, the firewall that we have diagrammed fits the definition of a perimeter firewall. This is the most common of all pfSense deployments.

How it works...

A **perimeter firewall** becomes the gatekeeper of all traffic flowing between interfaces. We will define firewall rules based on how we want that traffic to flow. A few common rules that most networks enforce are:

- **Allow all from LAN to WAN**: Allow users to get to the outside world so that they can surf the web, send e-mails, and so on.

- **Allow some from LAN to WAN**: A practice known as **egress filtering** involves limiting the types of traffic allowed to leave a network to ensure unauthorized or malicious traffic never leaves a network.

- **Block all from WAN to LAN**: Do not allow external users to get into our own private network.

- **Allow HTTP from LAN to DMZ**: Allow our internal users to access our company's webserver.

- **Allow HTTP from WAN to DMZ**: Allow external users to access our company's webserver.

- **Block all from DMZ to LAN**: Our DMZ is insecure since we're allowing external users to come in and access the web server. We want to protect ourselves by blocking any traffic that attempts to access our LAN from the DMZ.

pfSense also employs many advanced firewall features to accommodate the needs of more complex networks. pfSense is capable of:

- Supporting dozens of interfaces if necessary

- Handling multiple Internet connections, in case the primary Internet connection fails

- Fail-over protection, in case the primary firewall dies

- Load-balancing, to optimize network traffic by balancing demanding loads

There's more...

pfSense is highly flexible and can also be configured as any of the following devices. It's important to note that these roles are simply services that we will use within our perimeter firewall deployment, but larger environments may want to build these roles as separate machines to improve performance:

- **Router**: This is the second most common deployment of pfSense. A router determines a packet's destination and then sends it on its way, without applying any firewall rules.

▶ **VPN appliance**: A VPN server provides encrypted remote network connections. pfSense supports all the major virtual private networking protocols such as IPsec, PPTP, OpenVPN, and L2TP.

▶ **DHCP appliance**: A DHCP server assigns IP addresses to clients that request them.

▶ **DNS appliance**: A DNS server associates names with IP addresses. It's much easier to remember "google.com" than "173.194.33.104".

▶ **VoIP appliance**: **Voice over IP** (**VoIP**) is digital telephony, possible with pfSense using the FreeSWITCH package.

▶ **Sniffer appliance**: Sniffers analyze packets for patterns. This is often to detect and prevent traffic that attempts to exploit known vulnerabilities. pfSense utilizes the most widely deployed sniffer package in existence, Snort.

▶ **Wireless Access Point**: pfSense can be deployed strictly as a wireless access point.

pfSense can be configured with many more devices—pfSense being deployed as a special purpose appliance is only limited by the number of packages supported by the platform.

For more information, read through the PfSense online documentation:

Common Deployments

```
http://www.pfsense.org/index.php?option=com_content&ta
sk=view&id=71&Itemid=81
```

Determining our throughput requirements

This recipe will explain how to determine the throughput requirements, and subsequently the processing and memory requirements needed in our environment.

Getting ready

We'll want to prepare for determining our requirements by gathering the following information:

▶ Our Internet connection speed.

▶ Our network hardware speed. Will our network be capable of 10, 100, or 1000 Mbps speeds?

▶ What connection speeds will our different types of users be expecting?

How to do it...

1. Let's review the general throughput and feature guidelines (available at `http://pfsense.com/` at **Hardware | Selection & Sizing**):

Firewall throughput	Processing power required	Server hardware (PCI-X/PCI-e NICs)
10-20 Mbps	266-MHz CPU	No
21-50 Mbps	500-MHz CPU	No
51-200 Mbps	1-GHz CPU	No
201-500 Mbps	2-GHz CPU	Recommended
501+ Mbps	3-GHz CPU	Recommended

The following table defines any additional system requirements that would be necessary if deploying optional features:

Feature	Additional Requirements
VPN	A CPU's encrypted throughput is roughly 20 percent of its unencrypted throughput. If you have a 500-Mhz processor (~50 Mbps unencrypted) and you need more than 10 Mbps encrypted throughput, you're going to need a faster processor or a separate encryption card.
Captive portal	Environments with a larger number of captive portal users (100+) may need to bump their processing power slightly to achieve the same throughput.
Large state tables	The default state table size of 10,000 entries takes up 10 MB of RAM. Large environments with hundreds of thousands of entries will want to make sure they have the necessary memory available.
Squid Package	It is a package used for caching web content which requires extensive use of a hard disk with a large amount of storage. It is not for use with an embedded installation where writes to the compact flash card are kept to a minimum.
Snort Package	It is a packet sniffer/intrusion prevention and detection system (IPS/IDS). A minimum of 512 MB RAM is required.
NTop Package	A network traffic reporting tool. A minimum of 512 MB of RAM required.

2. Now, let's determine our own requirements:

   ❑ Our medium-sized business, *Any Company USA*, has 100 typical business users. Our network infrastructure consists of CAT5 cable and 100 Mbps switches. The majority of our traffic is web browsing, e-mails, and small file sharing. Our 100-Mbps Internet connection is ample, and our primary concern is being able to use what we're paying for.

   ❑ We want to provide VPN access for employees on the go, but we expect no more than a handful of VPN connections at any given time and throughput for these external users isn't a primary concern. Of the additional packages available to pfSense, we've decided we'd like to use the NTop package to help us analyze our traffic and identify problems.

         ❑   Lastly, given the money we're saving using the open source pfSense platform, we're going to build an additional fail-over firewall to comply with our organization's redundancy IT policy.

3. At this point we've identified our requirements as:

         ❑   1 Gbps network hardware (cables and switches)

         ❑   Unencrypted throughput of 100 Mbps

         ❑   Encrypted throughput (VPN) of 20 Mbps

         ❑   1-GHz CPU, 1-GB RAM

         ❑   A second identical machine to be used as a failover

How it works...

Throughput is the amount of data that can be processed at any given time. We may have a 100 Mbps fiber-optic Internet connection, but if our firewall's hardware can only process 20 Mbps, then that's all we're going to get.

Firewall throughput is only a factor for traffic *passing through* the firewall. Internet traffic meets this requirement (LAN <| WAN), as would any traffic between our own networks (LAN <| DMZ). However, traffic between two machines on the same network, 2 PCs in our LAN for example, won't be bottlenecked by the firewall.

There's more...

It's important to remember that certain firewall features have their own hardware requirements. For example, VPN connections require additional processing power and the Squid web-caching package isn't suitable for an embedded compact flash disk installation.

List of available packages

Unfortunately, a current list of packages available to pfSense isn't maintained online. Once pfSense is installed, we can view available packages in the **System | Packages** menu.

See also

▶   See Available Packages in *Appendix A, Monitoring and Logging*

▶   PfSense Official Documentation: Minimum Requirements

     `http://www.pfsense.org/index.php?option=com_content&task=view&id=45&Itemid=48`

▶   PfSense Official Documentation: Selection & Sizing

     `http://www.pfsense.org/index.php?option=com_content&task=view&id=52&Itemid=49`

Determining our interface requirements

This recipe will help us determine our interface requirements by analyzing our network design.

Getting ready

This recipe requires the analysis of our network diagram to understand how many interfaces our network will require. As an example, we'll be using my own home network diagram, which is a good example of a typical small office environment.

How to do it...

1. Let's analyze our network diagram:

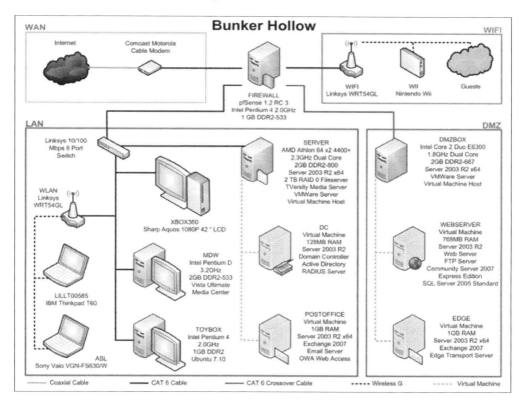

2. We can see that our environment consists of four separate interfaces:

- ❑ **WAN (Wide Area Network)**: The Internet.

- ❑ **LAN (Local Area Network)**: Our primary internal network.

- ❑ **DMZ (Demilitarized Zone)**: Our internal network we allow external access to. Web servers, e-mail servers, and any other externally accessible devices belong to this interface.

- ❑ **WiFi (Wireless Guest Network)**: We've created this network for the convenience of our guests. They can connect with an easy-to-remember password (or perhaps no password at all) and surf the Web. We consider this interface insecure and treat it as such. We will define rules so that it has no access to our other interfaces.

It's apparent that our firewall requires four **Network Interface Cards (NIC)**.

 Alternatively, the preceding diagram could be accomplished with two interfaces (WAN and LAN) and two VLANs (DMZ and WIFI).

How it works...

A firewall requires a separate NIC for every interface it hopes to support. This ensures a physical separation of network traffic. All inter-network traffic is forced to pass through the firewall where our rules will be applied and enforced. For that reason, a firewall requires a minimum of two NICs to function properly; one for internal traffic and one for external traffic. Each subsequent optional interface will require yet another NIC, which can be added at any time.

There's more...

Typically, an NIC will have a single Ethernet port. However, some NICs may have two, four, or even more Ethernet ports on a single card. Our firewall in the preceding scenario could have four single-port NICs or a single four-port network interface card. Either way, it works.

Single-port NIC	Four-port NIC

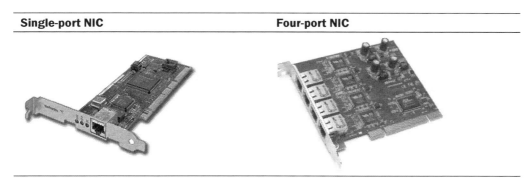

pfSense 2.0: Minimum interface requirements

New to the latest version of PfSense is a single interface minimum to install the system. This means that all interfaces are now optional, except for the WAN. This allows for more flexibility while building or upgrading the system, but a proper firewall still requires a minimum of two.

Choosing a standard or embedded Image

This recipe describes how to make the choice of using the standard or embedded version of pfSense.

Getting ready

Every standard feature of pfSense is supported on both the standard and embedded platforms but certain packages are not. The Squid web-caching package, for example, requires extensive writing to disk and should not be run on a compact flash drive.

How to do it...

1. Let's review the package we've chosen to install:

    NTop package: It is a traffic analysis tool. It requires a minimum of 512 KB RAM, but has no restrictions on the storage type.

2. Based on this and the convenience of compact flash cards, we're going to install the embedded version of pfSense.

How it works...

The standard image is meant to be installed on a hard drive. The embedded version is meant to be installed on a compact flash drive. Compact flash drives only have a limited number of writes during their lifespan and the embedded version of pfSense is designed to limit writes to the disk for this very reason. That being said, each platform has some distinct advantages and disadvantages:

Platform	Pros	Cons
Standard	All packages and features are supported	Entire drive must be overwritten (dual booting is not supported)
	Large amount of cheap storage space	Require larger power supply
Embedded	Fast access times	CF cards have a limited number of writes
	Cards can be easily swapped (backup, upgrades, and so on)	Not all packages are supported
	Requires little power	
	Silent	

There's more...

The installation disk for the standard version of pfSense is also a Live CD. If you'd just like to try pfSense out without installing it to any machine, you can run it live from the CD. You can even save your configuration to a floppy disk or USB drive. However, not all features are available while running pfSense from the Live CD.

See also

▶ pfSense online documentation: Versions

```
http://www.pfsense.org/index.php?option=com_content&task=view&i
d=43&Itemid=44
```

Choosing a Form Factor

This recipe describes how to choose the best hardware configuration based on our firewall requirements.

Getting ready

It's easiest to choose a form factor if we've already decided on the rest of our prerequisites:

- Deployment scenario
- Throughput requirements
- Interface requirements
- Image platform

How to do it...

Evaluate the different types of form factors:

1. **Small form**: Energy-efficient, quiet (often silent), small foot print form factor.
2. **Desktop**: Standard desktop hardware. Easily upgradable and most people will have an older machine lying around that's perfectly suited for running pfSense.
3. **Server**: Larger or more complex environments may require server class hardware.

Consider if any of our requirements require special hardware. In our case, we need moderate throughput and aren't using any packages that require special hardware. Low-power consumption and silent operation is important to our small office, so we're opting for small form factor.

How it works...

The choice of form factor has more to do with our environment than our pfSense installation. Every environment will vary and form factors will differ. Thanks to the vast variety of computer hardware on the market, any deployment of pfSense is possible on any type of form factor. While most standard platforms are installed on desktops, and most embedded platforms on appliances, there's no reason they can't be swapped if we've equipped our hardware properly.

There's more...

There's no reason we can't use a laptop! If we have an old laptop lying around, it would probably make a great, although unusual, pfSense machine. The biggest obstacle we'd likely face is adding additional NICs, but a USB Ethernet Adapter ought to work, although they are never recommended for production systems.

[As with all open-source projects, it's best to refer to the project's hardware compatibility list before adding new hardware.]

Installing the embedded platform on a desktop/server/laptop

Some people really enjoy the convenience of running a system from a compact flash card. Testing a new version of pfSense, or reverting back to a backup, is as easy as swapping CF cards. Most desktops don't come with a CF card reader installed, but there are plenty of adapters to choose from:

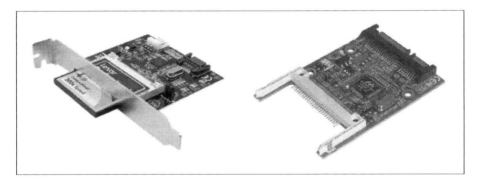

Installing the standard platform on an appliance

Of all the different installation scenarios, installing the standard version on an appliance equipped with a hard drive can be the most challenging. Appliances are meant to be small, so if they've already fit a hard drive in there you can bet there won't be an optical drive. Secondly, most appliances don't have built-in video-out which means another means of connection (usually serial or USB) is required.

We'll have to refer to our manufacturer's documentation if we find ourselves in this situation. There isn't much documentation available on the subject, but the pfSense guys have posted instructions on how to install the standard image on a Netgate Hamakua at `http://doc.pfsense.org/index.php/Full_install_on_Netgate_Hamakua`.

See also

- pfSense official documentation: Recommended Vendors

   `http://www.pfsense.org/index.php?option=com_content&task=view&id=44&Itemid=50`

Index

Thank you for buying
pfSense 2 Cookbook

About Packt Publishing

Packt, pronounced 'packed', published its first book "*Mastering phpMyAdmin for Effective MySQL Management*" in April 2004 and subsequently continued to specialize in publishing highly focused books on specific technologies and solutions.

Our books and publications share the experiences of your fellow IT professionals in adapting and customizing today's systems, applications, and frameworks. Our solution based books give you the knowledge and power to customize the software and technologies you're using to get the job done. Packt books are more specific and less general than the IT books you have seen in the past. Our unique business model allows us to bring you more focused information, giving you more of what you need to know, and less of what you don't.

Packt is a modern, yet unique publishing company, which focuses on producing quality, cutting-edge books for communities of developers, administrators, and newbies alike. For more information, please visit our website: www.packtpub.com.

About Packt Open Source

In 2010, Packt launched two new brands, Packt Open Source and Packt Enterprise, in order to continue its focus on specialization. This book is part of the Packt Open Source brand, home to books published on software built around Open Source licences, and offering information to anybody from advanced developers to budding web designers. The Open Source brand also runs Packt's Open Source Royalty Scheme, by which Packt gives a royalty to each Open Source project about whose software a book is sold.

Writing for Packt

We welcome all inquiries from people who are interested in authoring. Book proposals should be sent to author@packtpub.com. If your book idea is still at an early stage and you would like to discuss it first before writing a formal book proposal, contact us; one of our commissioning editors will get in touch with you.

We're not just looking for published authors; if you have strong technical skills but no writing experience, our experienced editors can help you develop a writing career, or simply get some additional reward for your expertise.

open source

community experience distilled

Beginning OpenVPN 2.0.9

Beginning OpenVPN 2.0.9

ISBN: 978-1-847197-06-1   Paperback: 356 pages

Build and integrate Virtual Private Networks using OpenVPN

1. A practical guide to using OpenVPN for building both basic and complex Virtual Private Networks (VPNs)

2. Learn how to make use of OpenVPNs modules, high-end-encryption and how to combine it with servers for your individual privacy

3. Advanced management of security certificates

4. Get to know the new features of the forthcoming version 2.1 of OpenVPN

Silverlight 4 User Interface Cookbook

Silverlight 4 User Interface Cookbook

ISBN: 978-1-847198-86-0   Paperback: 280 pages

Build and implement rich, standard-friendly user interfaces with Silverlight and Expression Blend

1. The first and only book to focus exclusively on Silverlight UI development.

2. Have your applications stand out from the crowd with leading, innovative, and friendly user interfaces.

3. Real world projects which you can explore in detail and make modifications as you go.

Please check **www.PacktPub.com** for information on our titles

open source
community experience distilled

NHibernate 3.0
Cookbook

70 incredibly powerful recipes for using the full spectrum
of solutions in the NHibernate ecosystem

Jason Dentler

NHibernate 3.0 Cookbook

ISBN: 978-1-849513-04-3   Paperback: 328 pages

Get solutions to common NHibernate problems to
develop high-quality performance-critical data access
applications

1. Master the full range of NHibernate features

2. Reduce hours of application development time
   and get better application architecture and
   performance

3. Create, maintain, and update your database
   structure automatically with the help of
   NHibernate

Joomla!
Web Security

Secure your Joomla! website from common security threats with
this easy-to-use guide

Tom Canavan

PACKT

Joomla! Web Security

ISBN: 978-1-847194-88-6   Paperback: 264 pages

Secure your Joomla! website from common security
threats with this easy-to-use guide

1. Learn how to secure your Joomla! websites

2. Real-world tools to protect against hacks on your
   site

3. Implement disaster recovery features

4. Set up SSL on your site

5. Covers Joomla! 1.0 as well as 1.5

Please check **www.PacktPub.com** for information on our titles

13960447R00144

Made in the USA
Lexington, KY
01 March 2012